Cambridge Experience Readers

Level 5

Series editor: Nicholas T

Sherlock

by Sir Arthur Conan Doyle

Retold by Richard MacAndrew

CAMBRIDGE
UNIVERSITY PRESS

CAMBRIDGE
UNIVERSITY PRESS

University Printing House, Cambridge CB2 8BS, United Kingdom

Cambridge University Press is part of the University of Cambridge.

It furthers the University's mission by disseminating knowledge in the pursuit of education, learning and research at the highest international levels of excellence.

www.cambridge.org
Information on this title: www.cambridge.org/9781107621862

© Cambridge University Press 2014

First published 2014
Reprinted 2016

Richard MacAndrew has asserted his right to be identified as the Author of the Work in accordance with the Copyright, Design and Patents Act 1988.

Printed in Italy by Rotolito Lombarda S.p.A.

ISBN 978-110-7621-86-2 Paperback; legal deposit: M-7296-2014

No character in this work is based on any person living or dead.
Any resemblance to an actual person or situation is purely accidental.

Illustrations by Antonio Salazar

Audio recording by BraveArts

Typeset by Óscar Latorre

Contents

People in the story

Sherlock Holmes: the famous detective
Dr Watson: Sherlock Holmes's friend and assistant
Mycroft Holmes: Sherlock Holmes's brother
Arthur Cadogan West: works at the Woolwich Arsenal
Miss Violet Westbury: Cadogan West's fiancée
Inspector Lestrade: a police inspector
Sir James Walter: a government expert
Colonel Valentine Walter: Sir James's brother
Sidney Johnson: a technical engineer at the Woolwich Arsenal
Hugo Oberstein: a foreign agent

BEFORE YOU READ

1 What do you know about Sherlock Holmes?

2 Where do you think the story takes place?

3 Look at the pictures on pages 5–43 and *People in the story* above. Who do you think the people are?

The Bruce-Partington Plans

It was the third week of November and a thick yellow fog had settled over London. From the Monday to the Thursday it had rarely been possible from our windows in Baker Street to see even the houses across the street. The first three of these days, Holmes had been patiently studying a subject which had been his hobby for some time – the music of the Middle Ages. But when, for the fourth time, we pushed back our chairs from breakfast and saw the heavy brown mist outside the windows, my friend's impatient and active personality could no longer take this dull existence. He wandered restlessly around our sitting room; he bit his nails; he tapped the furniture nervously; and he complained about the inactivity.

'Nothing of interest in the paper, Watson?' he said.

I realised that by anything of interest, Holmes was asking about anything of *criminal* interest. There was the news of a revolution, of a possible war, and of a likely change of government. However, these were of little interest to my companion. The only criminal reports I could find were very ordinary. Holmes sighed impatiently and continued to wander around the room.

'The London criminal is certainly a dull person,' he said, sounding like a hunter who can find nothing to shoot. 'Look out of this window, Watson. See how people suddenly appear, are briefly seen, and then quickly disappear once more into the mist. On a day like this, a thief or a murderer could stroll round London like a tiger in the jungle. No one would see him until he made his move.'

'There have,' I said, 'been a large number of small robberies.'

Holmes muttered something rude and then turned towards me.

'My abilities demand something far more worthy than that,' he said. 'It is fortunate for this community that I am not a criminal.'

'It certainly is!' I agreed enthusiastically.

'Imagine that I had a good reason to want to kill someone,' continued Holmes. 'How easy it would be on a day like this! I could suggest a meeting, I could make up an appointment, and it would all be over. It is just as well they don't have days of fog in countries where murder is common.'

There was the sound of someone knocking.

'At last!' cried Holmes. 'Here comes something to bring some excitement into our lives.'

He rushed over to open the door. It was the postman with a telegram[1]. Holmes tore it open and before long burst out laughing.

'Well, well! I don't believe it!' he said. 'My brother Mycroft is coming round.'

'And so ...?' I asked.

'And so ...?' said Holmes. 'It is like coming across a train in the middle of the road. Mycroft has his rails and he stays on them. His home in Pall Mall, his club, his office in Whitehall – that is where you find him. Once, and only once, has he been here. What disaster can have knocked him off his rails?'

'Doesn't he explain?' I asked.

Holmes handed me his brother's telegram.

Must see you about Cadogan West. Coming at once. Mycroft.

'Cadogan West?' I said. I had heard that name.

'It means nothing to me,' said Holmes. 'But it is extraordinary that Mycroft should do something so out of character. The moon might as well stop going round the earth. By the way, do you know what Mycroft does?'

'You told me once that he had some minor position in the British government.'

Holmes laughed.

'I didn't know you quite so well then,' explained Holmes. 'You have to be careful when talking about government affairs. You're right in thinking that he works for the government. You'd also be right in a way if you said that occasionally he *is* the government.'

'What!' I said. 'But how?'

'Well, Mycroft has the tidiest and most organised brain you can imagine,' replied Holmes, wandering up and down the room again. 'He can store more facts than any other man alive. The same great powers which I use as a crime detective he uses for the government. Mycroft collects information from every government department. He's the only person with an overview of everything that's happening in government. Only he can see the full effect that different courses of action will have. Again and again his word has been responsible for major decisions.'

Holmes stopped walking around and then continued.

'But he's on his way here. What on earth can it mean? Who is Cadogan West, and why is Mycroft interested in him?'

'I've got it,' I shouted. And I searched quickly through the pile of newspapers on the sofa. 'Yes, here it is! Cadogan West was the young man who was found dead on the Underground on Tuesday morning.'

Holmes sat up straight, his pipe halfway to his lips.

'This must be serious, Watson,' said Holmes. 'A death which has caused my brother to change his habits cannot be ordinary. What in the world can Mycroft have to do with it? The case was unremarkable as I remember it. The young man apparently fell out of a train and killed himself. He had not been robbed, and there was no particular reason to suspect violence. Isn't that right?'

'There has been an inquest[2],' I said, 'and a good many fresh facts have come out. Looking at it more closely, I should certainly say that it's a curious case.'

'Judging by its effect on my brother, it must be a most extraordinary one.' Holmes made himself comfortable in his armchair. 'Now, Watson, tell me the facts.'

'The man's name was Arthur Cadogan West,' I told him. 'He was twenty-seven years old, engaged to be married, and worked in an office at the Woolwich Arsenal[3].'

'A government employee,' said Holmes. 'That must be why Mycroft is interested!'

'Cadogan West left Woolwich suddenly on Monday night,' I continued. 'He was last seen by his fiancée, Miss Violet Westbury, who he left suddenly in the fog at about 7:30 that evening. There had been no argument between them and she can give no reason for his action. The next thing heard of him was when his dead body was discovered in London by a railway inspector named Mason, just outside Aldgate Station on the Underground train line.'

'When?' asked Holmes.

'The body was found at six on Tuesday morning,' I replied. 'It was lying by the rails close to the station, where the line comes out of a tunnel. The head was badly damaged – an injury which might well have been caused by a fall from the train. The body could only have got on the line that way. If someone had carried the body down there, they would have gone past the ticket collector at the station. This point seems absolutely certain.'

'Very good,' said Holmes. 'So the man, dead or alive, either fell or was thrown from a train. That much is clear. Go on.'

'The young man was travelling from east to west at some late hour of the night. However, it's impossible to say when and where he got on the train.'

'His ticket, of course, would show that.'

'There was no ticket in his pockets.'

'No ticket!' said Holmes. 'Dear me, Watson, this is very unusual. From my experience, it is not possible to reach an Underground platform without showing a ticket. Presumably, then, the young man had one. Was it taken from him in order to keep secret the station he came from? It is possible. Or did he drop it in the train? That's also possible. I understand that there was no sign of robbery?'

'Apparently not,' I replied. 'There's a list here of his possessions: his wallet, containing a small amount of money; two tickets for the Woolwich Theatre, dated that evening; and a small packet of technical[4] papers.'

'There it is at last, Watson!' said Holmes with a satisfied look on his face. 'The government – Woolwich Arsenal – technical papers – my brother Mycroft – the chain is complete. But, if I am not mistaken, here he comes.'

A moment later the large figure of Mycroft Holmes entered the room. Tall and heavily built, his deep grey eyes were full of understanding, and his expression intelligent.

Close behind Mycroft was our old friend Inspector Lestrade, of Scotland Yard[5] – a thin and hard man. The seriousness of both their faces suggested this was a weighty problem. Mycroft Holmes sat down heavily in an armchair.

'A most annoying business, Sherlock,' he said. 'I hate changing my habits, but I was given no choice. This is a real crisis. I have never seen the Prime Minister so upset. Have you read about the case?'

'We have just done so. What were the technical papers found on Cadogan West's body?' replied Holmes.

'Ah, that's the point! Fortunately, the news hasn't got out. The press would be furious if it did. The papers which this sorry young man had in his pocket were the plans for the Bruce-Partington submarine[6],' said Mycroft.

His brother and I waited for him to continue.

'Surely you have heard of it?' asked Mycroft.

'Only by name,' replied Holmes.

'You cannot overestimate its importance,' explained Mycroft. 'It has been the most jealously guarded of all government secrets. Believe me – the Bruce-Partington submarine is the most important development that the navy[7] has ever seen. The plans are extremely complicated and every effort has been made to keep them secret. There are thirty separate new inventions, each of which is essential to the working of the whole. The only copy of the plans is kept in a special safe[8] in a private office next to the arsenal. There are strong locks on all the doors and windows. Under no circumstances were the plans ever to be taken out of the office. And yet here we find them in the pocket of a dead junior office worker in the heart of London. It's simply awful.'

'But – the plans – they have now been returned to you?' said Holmes.

'No, Sherlock, no! That's the problem,' replied Mycroft, 'We don't have all of them. Ten papers were taken from Woolwich. There were seven in the pocket of Cadogan West. The three most important are gone – stolen, disappeared. You must stop everything else, Sherlock. This is an urgent international problem, which you must solve. Why did Cadogan West take the papers? Where are the missing ones? How did he die? How can this wrong be put right? Find an answer to these questions, and you will have done a good service for your country.'

My friend smiled.

'Well,' he said. 'The problem certainly presents some points of interest, and I shall be very pleased to look into it. Some more facts, please.'

'I've noted down the more essential ones here,' said Mycroft, handing Holmes a sheet of paper. 'And I've noted down a few addresses which you will find useful. The person who is responsible for the papers is the famous government expert, Sir James Walter. He's a man whose love for his country is above suspicion. He's one of two people who have a key to the safe. I should add that the papers were definitely in the office during working hours on Monday, and that Sir James left for London at about three o'clock, taking his key with him. He was a guest at a house at Barclay Square for the whole of that evening.'

'Are you sure that's true?' asked Holmes.

'Yes,' replied Mycroft. 'His brother, Colonel Valentine Walter, witnessed him leave Woolwich, and Admiral Sinclair saw him arrive in London.'

'Who is the other man with a key?'

'The senior technical engineer, Mr Sidney Johnson. He's a man of forty, married, with five children. He's a silent, unsmiling man. However, he has, generally speaking, an excellent record in public service. He's unpopular with his colleagues, but he is a hard worker. According to him, he was at home the whole of Monday evening – although we only have his wife's word for that. And he says his key never left his pocket.'

'Tell us about Cadogan West,' said Holmes.

'He'd worked for the government for ten years,' replied Mycroft. 'He was a good worker. People sometimes felt he was impatient and rather superior, but a straight, honest man. He sat next to Sidney Johnson in the office. His duties meant that he personally worked with the plans every day. No one else touched them.'

'Who locked up the plans that night?' asked Holmes.

'Mr Sidney Johnson,' answered Mycroft.

'Well, it is surely perfectly clear who took them away. They were actually found on Cadogan West. That seems final, does it not?'

'It does, Sherlock,' replied Mycroft. 'And yet it leaves so much unexplained. In the first place, why did he take them?'

'Can you suggest any possible reason for taking the papers to London except to sell them to a foreign agent?' asked Holmes.

'No, I cannot.'

'Then, for the moment,' began Holmes, 'let us believe that this is what happened. Young West took the papers. Now he could only do this by having a copy of the key ...'

'Copies of several keys,' interrupted Mycroft. 'He had to open the building and the room too.'

'He had, then, copies of several keys,' continued Holmes. 'He took the papers to London to sell the ideas in them. No doubt he intended to put them back in the safe the next morning before they were missed. However, while in London on this dishonourable business he met his end.'

'We can't invent a better explanation with what we know at the moment,' said Mycroft. 'But, Sherlock, think how much you leave unexplained. Let us suppose that young Cadogan West actually had decided to take these papers to London. He would then presumably have made an appointment with the foreign agent and kept his evening free. Instead, he bought two tickets for the theatre, got halfway there with his fiancée, and suddenly disappeared.'

Holmes watched his brother through half-closed eyes.

'That is the first objection to your explanation,' continued Mycroft. 'And objection No. 2: let's suppose that he reaches London and sees the foreign agent. He must replace the papers before morning or the loss will be discovered. He took away ten papers. Only seven were found in his pocket. What happened to the other three? He certainly wouldn't leave them anywhere. And, again, where is his payment for this dishonourable act? Surely we'd expect to find a large amount of money in his pocket.'

'It seems perfectly clear to me,' said Inspector Lestrade. 'He took the papers to sell them. He saw the foreign agent. They could not agree on the price. Cadogan West started home again, but the agent went with him. In the train the agent murdered him, took the more essential papers, and threw Cadogan West's body out of the train. That would explain everything, wouldn't it?'

'Why wasn't a ticket found on the body?' asked Mycroft.

'The ticket would have shown which station was nearest the agent's house,' answered Lestrade. 'Therefore he took it from the murdered man's pocket.'

'Good, Lestrade, very good,' said Holmes. 'Your idea is well thought out. But if this is true, then the case is at an end. The thief is dead and the plans of the Bruce-Partington submarine are presumably already out of the country. What is there for us to do?'

'We must act, Sherlock. We must act!' cried Mycroft, jumping to his feet. 'I strongly suspect this is not what happened. Use your powers! Go to the scene of the crime! See the people involved! Stop at nothing! In all your career you have never had so great a chance to serve your country.'

'Well, well!' said Holmes, looking rather unconcerned. 'Come, Watson! And you, Lestrade. Would you care to join us? We'll begin our investigation at Aldgate Station. Goodbye, Mycroft. I will report to you by this evening. But I warn you in advance that you should not expect too much.'

An hour later Holmes, Lestrade and I stood in the Underground where the rails come out of the tunnel just before Aldgate Station. A polite red-faced old gentleman from the railway company was with us.

'This is where the young man's body was found,' he said, pointing to a spot near the rails. 'It couldn't have fallen from above because there are no holes in the roof of the tunnel – as you can see. Therefore, it could only have come from a train. And, as far as we can work out, that train must have come through here at about midnight on Monday.'

'Has the train been examined for any sign of violence?' asked Holmes.

'There were no signs of violence, and no ticket was found,' replied the railwayman.

'We did get some fresh information this morning,' said Lestrade. 'A passenger who went through Aldgate at about 11:40 on Monday night said that he heard a strange noise just before the train reached the station. He said it could have been a body hitting the railway line. There was thick fog, however, and he couldn't see anything. He made no report of it at the time.'

Lestrade looked at Holmes.

'Why, whatever is the matter, Holmes?' he asked.

My friend was standing and staring at the rails, where they came round the corner out of the tunnel. There was an expression of deep thought on his face. Aldgate is a junction, where many lines meet. Holmes's keen, questioning eyes were fixed on the points⁹. I saw on his face that tightening of the lips, that movement of the nostrils, and the concentration of the heavy eyebrows which I knew so well.

'The points,' he said quietly.

'What about the points? What do you mean?' asked Lestrade.

'I don't suppose there are many points on a line like this?' asked Holmes.

'Very few,' replied the railwayman.

'And a corner, too,' said Holmes thoughtfully. 'Points, and a corner. Perhaps I could be right!'

'What is it, Mr Holmes?' asked the railwayman. 'Have you found a clue?'

'An idea,' replied Holmes. 'Nothing more than that. But the case certainly grows in interest. It is most unusual. And yet why shouldn't it be?'

He looked at the rails again.

'Was there blood on the line?' he asked.

'Hardly any,' replied the railwayman.

'But I understand that there was considerable damage to the body.'

'Bones were broken, but there was little damage to the outside of the body,' replied the man.

'And yet you would have expected some bleeding,' said Holmes. 'Would it be possible for me to examine the train?'

'I'm afraid not, Mr Holmes,' replied the man. 'The carriages[10] have already been separated and used to make up new trains for the weekend.'

'You can be certain, Mr Holmes,' said Lestrade, 'that every carriage was looked at very carefully. I organised it myself.'

'As it happens, it was not the carriages that I wanted to examine,' said Holmes, turning away impatiently. 'Watson, we have done all we can here. We need not take up any more of your time, Mr Lestrade. I think our investigations must now take us to Woolwich.'

At London Bridge, Holmes called his brother, asking him to send to Baker Street a complete list of all foreign spies or international agents known to be in England.

His face still wore an expression of keenness and restless energy as we took our seats on the Woolwich train. Some new and important circumstance had obviously opened up a creative line of thought. Think of a hunting dog with its ears and tail hanging down, as it lies around all day and sleeps – that was Holmes this morning. Now he was the same dog, powerful and with bright eyes, speeding after the smell of a fox or a rabbit.

'There are clues here. There are possibilities,' he said. 'I should have seen them and understood them.'

'Well, I'm still wandering around in the dark,' I said.

'The end of the road is dark to me too,' he replied. 'But I've got an idea which may take us a long way down it. The man was killed somewhere else, and his body was on the *roof* of the train.'

'On the roof!'

'Remarkable, isn't it?' said Holmes. 'But consider the facts. Was it by chance that the body was found at exactly the spot where the train rolls from side to side as it comes round on the points? Isn't that the place where something on the roof might fall off? The points would not affect anything inside the train. So, either the body fell off the roof, or something very curious has happened. And then consider the question of the blood. Of course, there would have been no bleeding on the line if the body had already bled somewhere else. Each fact is interesting in itself. But put them together …'

'And the ticket, too!' I cried.

'Exactly,' agreed Holmes. 'It explains the absence of a ticket. Everything fits together.'

'But if this is what happened,' I said, 'we're still as far as ever from solving the mystery of his death. In fact, it becomes stranger rather than simpler.'

'Perhaps,' said Holmes thoughtfully. He looked out of the window in silence until the train arrived at last at Woolwich Station. There he called a taxi and took Mycroft's list of addresses from his pocket.

'We have a number of calls to make in Woolwich this afternoon,' he said. 'I think that Sir James Walter should be the first.'

The famous Sir James lived in a fine house with lovely gardens stretching down to the Thames. As we reached it, the fog was lifting, and a thin, watery sunshine was breaking through. A servant[11] answered the door.

When we asked to see Sir James, the servant replied, with an unhappy look on his face, 'I'm afraid Sir James died this morning.'

'Good God!' cried Holmes in amazement. 'How did he die?'

'Perhaps you would care to come in, sir, and see his brother, Colonel Valentine?' suggested the servant.

'An excellent idea,' replied Holmes.

The servant showed us into a rather dark sitting room. A moment later we were joined by a tall, handsome, light-bearded man of about fifty – the younger brother of the dead man. His wild eyes, tearful cheeks, and untidy hair were all signs of the sudden disaster which had hit this household. He found it very difficult to speak.

'It was this horrible affair of the missing papers,' he said. 'My brother, Sir James, was a man of great honour. He couldn't go on after something like this. It broke his heart. He was always so proud of his department. It was a terrible shock.'

'We were hoping that he might have given us some ideas which would have helped us to clear the matter up,' explained Holmes.

'It was all a mystery to him,' replied Colonel Valentine, 'just as it is to all of us. He had already told the police everything he knew. Naturally he had no doubt that Cadogan West was guilty.'

'You have no new information about the affair?' asked Holmes.

'I don't know anything myself except what I have read or heard. I don't wish to be impolite, Mr Holmes, but you will understand that we are very upset at present. I must ask you to leave.'

'This is indeed an unexpected development,' said my friend when we had got back in the taxi. 'I wonder if the death was natural, or whether the poor man killed himself! If he killed himself, maybe he was punishing himself because his department lost the papers. We must leave that question for another day. Now let's visit the Cadogan Wests.'

Cadogan West's mother lived in a small but well-kept house on the edge of Woolwich. The old lady was too affected by her son's death to be of any help. However, at her side was a white-faced young lady, who introduced herself as Miss Violet Westbury, the fiancée of the dead man. She had been the last person to see him on that terrible night.

'I can't explain it, Mr Holmes,' she said. 'I haven't slept since that night. I've been thinking night and day about what really happened. Arthur was the most determined, polite man on earth. He loved his country dearly. An accusation that he stole anything is ridiculous, impossible, unbelievable. Anyone who knew him would say that.'

'But the facts, Miss Westbury?' said Holmes.

'Yes, yes,' agreed Miss Westbury. 'I admit I can't explain them.'

'Was he in need of money?' asked Holmes.

'No,' replied Miss Westbury. 'His needs were very simple and his salary sufficient. He'd saved a few hundred pounds, and we were going to get married in the New Year.'

'He showed no signs of stress?' asked Holmes. Then he added, 'Miss Westbury, you must be absolutely honest with us.'

The quick eye of my companion had noticed some change in her manner. She coloured and did not speak for a moment.

'Yes,' she said at last, 'I had a feeling that there was something on his mind.'

'For long?'

'Only for the last week or so. He was thoughtful and worried. Once I tried to persuade him to tell me about it. He admitted that there was something, and that it was to do with his work. "It's too serious for me to speak about, even to you," he said. He wouldn't say anything else.'

'Now tell us about that last evening,' said Holmes.

'We were going to the theatre,' she replied. 'The fog was incredibly thick. We were walking, and our route took us close to the office. Suddenly he rushed off into the fog.'

'Without a word?' asked Holmes.

'A small shout,' she replied. 'That was all. I waited, but he never returned. Then I walked home. Next morning, after the office at Woolwich Arsenal opened, some of his colleagues came to ask where he was. At about twelve o'clock we heard the terrible news. Oh, Mr Holmes, if you could only, only save his honour! It was so much to him.'

Holmes gave the poor lady a sad look.

'Come, Watson,' he said. 'We must move on. Our next stop will be the office where the papers were taken from.'

We said our goodbyes and returned to our taxi.

'The case against this young man was black enough before, but our inquiries are making it blacker,' he commented as the taxi set off. 'His intended marriage gives him a motive for the crime. He naturally wanted money. The idea was in his head, since he spoke about it. And he nearly involved the girl in the crime by telling her his plans. It's all very bad.'

'But surely, Holmes, his good character must count for something?' I argued. 'And why would he leave the girl in the street and rush off to commit a crime?'

'Exactly!' said Holmes. 'There are certainly objections. Nevertheless it's a powerful case.'

Mr Sidney Johnson, the senior technical engineer, met us at the Woolwich office. He was a thin, middle-aged man with glasses. He rubbed his hands together nervously.

'This is bad, Mr Holmes, very bad!' he said. 'Have you heard about Sir James's death?'

'We've just come from his house,' replied Holmes.

'Good God!' he said. 'It's awful to think that West, of all people, should have stolen the plans!'

'You're sure he's guilty, then?' asked Holmes.

'I can see no other explanation,' replied Johnson. 'And yet I would have trusted him as I trust myself.'

'What time was the office closed on Monday?' asked Holmes.

'Five o'clock,' answered Johnson.

'Did you close it?' asked Holmes.

'I'm always the last man to leave,' replied Johnson.

'Where were the plans?' asked Holmes.

'In the safe. I put them there myself,' said Johnson.

'If Cadogan West wanted to get into the building after hours,' said Holmes, 'he would need three keys, wouldn't he, before he could reach the papers?'

'Yes, he would,' replied Johnson. 'The key to the outside door, the key to the office, and the key to the safe.'

'And only Sir James Walter and you had those keys?' asked Holmes.

'I have no keys to the doors,' replied Johnson, 'only to the safe.'

'Was Sir James a tidy, organised man?' asked Holmes.

'Yes, I think he was,' replied Johnson. 'I know that he always kept those three keys on the same ring. I have often seen them there.'

'And that ring went with him to London?' said Holmes.

'That's what he said.'

'And your key never left your pocket?'

'Never.'

'Then if West is guilty, he must have had copies of the keys,' said Holmes. 'And yet there were no keys found on his body.'

Holmes thought for a moment.

'One other point,' he said. 'If someone in this office wanted to sell the plans, wouldn't it be simpler to copy them rather than to take the originals?'

'You'd need considerable technical knowledge to copy the plans properly,' replied Johnson.

'But would I be right in thinking that Sir James, and you, and Cadogan West all had that technical knowledge?' said Holmes.

'No doubt we had,' replied Johnson. 'But what's the point of thinking like that when the original plans were actually found on West?'

'Well, it's certainly strange that he should risk taking the originals,' began Holmes, 'especially if he could safely have made copies, which would have been just as valuable.'

'No doubt it is strange,' replied Johnson. 'And yet that's what he did.'

'Every inquiry in this case uncovers something that cannot be explained,' commented Holmes, before changing the subject. 'Now there are three papers still missing. They are, as I understand, the essential ones.'

'That's right.'

'Do you mean that anyone holding those three papers, but without the seven others, could build a Bruce-Partington submarine?' asked Holmes.

'That's what I originally thought,' replied Johnson. 'However, today I have looked at the seven papers that were returned, and now I'm not so sure. One of the new inventions used in the submarine is on one of those seven papers. Until someone could create that piece of equipment for themselves they wouldn't be able to make the boat. Of course they might soon solve that problem.'

'But the three missing drawings are the most important?' asked Holmes.

'Without doubt,' said Johnson.

'I think, with your permission,' said Holmes, 'I'll now have a look round this office.'

Holmes examined the lock on the safe, the door of the room, and finally the shutters that closed in front of each window. It was only when we were in the garden outside that he became excited. There was a bush outside the window, and several of the branches had been broken. He examined these carefully, and then studied some marks on the earth beneath. Finally he asked Mr Johnson to close the shutters. He showed me that they hardly met in the middle, and that it would be possible for anyone outside to see what was going on inside the room.

'Well, Watson,' he then said, 'I do not think that Woolwich can help us further. Let's see if we can do better in London.'

We did, however, gather one more piece of information at Woolwich Station. The man in the ticket office knew Cadogan West well by sight. He told us that he had seen Cadogan West on the Monday night, and that he had gone to London on the 8:15 train to London Bridge. He was alone and took a single ticket. The man noticed at the time that Cadogan West seemed nervous and excited. A look at the timetable showed us that the 8:15 was the first train he could have taken after leaving Miss Westbury at about 7:30.

'Let's try and work out what happened, Watson,' said Holmes after half an hour of silence. 'In all our joint adventures I do not think that we have ever had a case which was more difficult to understand. Every time we make a fresh advance, there just seems to be another hill to climb. However, I am certain we have made some important progress.'

Holmes looked thoughtful and then spoke again: 'Our inquiries at Woolwich have mainly led us to believe in the guilt of young Cadogan West. However, the clues at the office window would lend themselves to a more optimistic explanation. Let us suppose, for example, that West was approached by some foreign agent. He might have had to promise to keep such a discussion secret. However, it would almost certainly have affected him in the way that his fiancée told us, making him thoughtful and worried. Let's also suppose that as Cadogan West was on his way to the theatre with the young lady, he suddenly, in the fog, caught sight of this same foreign agent going in the direction of the Woolwich office. The only thing he could think of was that he had to do his duty. He followed the man. He looked through the office window. He witnessed the documents being stolen. In this way we avoid the argument that no one would take the originals when they could make copies. This foreign agent had to take originals. So far the story makes sense.'

'What is the next step?' I asked.

'Then we come into difficulties. One would imagine that in such circumstances the first act of young Cadogan West would be to grab the thief and raise the alarm. Why didn't he? Could it instead have been a colleague, one of his superiors, who took the papers? That would explain West's behaviour. Or could the thief have escaped in the fog? West therefore set off at once to London to catch him at his house – if, indeed, he knew where the thief lived. He must have felt that the situation was extremely urgent, since he left his girlfriend standing in the fog and made no effort to communicate with her. Our story stops there. And it's a long way to get from there to someone putting West's body, with seven papers in his pocket, on the roof of an Underground train. My feeling now is that we should work from the other end of the time line. If Mycroft has sent us the list of foreign agents I asked for earlier, we may be able to choose the right man and follow two lines of inquiry instead of one.'

Sure enough, there was a note waiting for us at Baker Street. Holmes looked at it quickly and threw it over to me.

There are only two men who would get involved with an affair as big as this. They are: Louis La Rothiere, of Campden Mansions, Notting Hill; and Hugo Oberstein, 13 Caulfield Gardens, Kensington. We know Oberstein was in town on Monday, but he is now reported to have left. Glad to hear you have seen some light. The Prime Minister is waiting anxiously for your final report. The whole force of the government is ready to help if you should need it. Mycroft.

Excitedly Holmes spread out his big map of London. 'Well, well,' he said presently, making a satisfied noise, 'I do honestly believe that we are going to succeed after all.' He banged his hand against my shoulder with sudden good humour. 'I'm going out now. Just to have a look around. I won't attempt anything serious without my trusty friend and biographer. I will be back in an hour or two.'

Some of Holmes's happiness passed itself on to me. He never gave up his usual seriousness of manner without good cause. I waited impatiently for his return all through that long November evening. At last, soon after nine o'clock, he rang telling me to meet him at Goldini's Restaurant in Kensington. I was to take some tools, a torch and my gun.

This was not sensible equipment for a respectable person to carry through the dark, foggy streets. I hid it all carefully in my overcoat and went straight to the address he had given me. I found my friend sitting at a little round table near the door of a bright Italian restaurant.

'Have you brought the tools?' he asked.

'They're here, in my overcoat,' I replied.

'Excellent,' he said. 'Now it must be obvious to you, Watson, that the young man's body was *placed* on the roof of the train.'

'Couldn't he have been dropped from a bridge?' I asked.

'I'd say it was impossible,' answered Holmes. 'If you examine the roofs of underground trains, you'll find that they are round, and there's no rail along the sides to stop a body falling off. Therefore, we can say for certain that young Cadogan West was placed on the roof of the train.'

'How could he be placed there?' I asked.

'There's only one possible way. You know that the Underground runs clear of tunnels at some places in the city. When I've travelled on it, I've occasionally seen windows just above my head. Now, let's suppose that a train stopped under one of these windows. Would there be any difficulty in placing a body on the roof?'

'It seems most unlikely,' I replied.

'We must fall back on the old saying,' said Holmes. 'When all other explanations fail, whatever remains, however improbable, must be the truth. In this case all other explanations *have* failed. When I found that the leading foreign agent, who had just left London, lived in a row of houses right next to the Underground, I was delighted.'

'Indeed.'

'Yes,' said Holmes. 'Mr Hugo Oberstein, of 13 Caulfield Gardens, became the focus of my attention. I began my investigations at Gloucester Road Station, where a very helpful man from the railway company took me along the line. We discovered that a window on the back stairs at Caulfield Gardens opens over the line. He also let me check an even more essential fact: Underground trains frequently stop for some minutes at that very spot because there is a junction with other railways.'

'Fantastic, Holmes! You've done it!' I said.

'So far, Watson. So far. We're advancing, but the goal is still some way away,' said Holmes. 'Having seen the back of Caulfield Gardens, I visited the front and satisfied myself that Oberstein was not there. We must remember that Oberstein has gone abroad to get rid of the plans. However, he's not 'on the run' because at the moment he has no reason to fear the police. I'm sure the idea of a couple of ordinary people paying his house a visit would never have occurred to him. So that is exactly what we are about to do.'

'Couldn't we speak to the police about what we have discovered and let them take over now?' I asked.

'There's not enough evidence.'

'What else can we hope to find?'

'We cannot tell what may be there.'

'I don't like it, Holmes.'

'My dear old friend,' said Holmes, 'you can keep watch in the street. I'll do the criminal part. This is not a time to worry about details. We have to go.'

My answer was to stand up.

'You are right, Holmes,' I said. 'We have to go.'

He jumped up and shook me by the hand.

'I knew you'd come,' he said, and for a moment I saw something in his eyes – something nearer to fondness than I had ever seen before.

13 Caulfield Gardens was a large house in west London. Holmes shone his torch at the huge front door.

'This is a serious piece of work,' he said. 'It certainly has more than one lock. We'll do better at the back door.' A minute later we were there, and Holmes set to work. I saw him lean into it and push hard. Then with a sharp crash it flew open. We found ourselves in a dark corridor and closed the door behind us. Holmes led the way up an uncarpeted stair. Then the dull yellow light from his torch picked out a low window.

'Here we are, Watson,' he said. 'This must be the window.' He threw it open, and as he did so there was a low sound, growing steadily louder and louder until a train rushed deafeningly past us in the darkness. Holmes flashed his light along the bottom of the window. There was a thick coat of coal dust over it from the passing trains, but the black surface was marked and rubbed in places.

'You can see where they rested the body,' said Holmes. 'Oh! Watson! Look at this! There can be no doubt that it is a blood mark.'

He was pointing to some faint coloured marks along the edge of the window. 'Here is another on the stone of the stair. The demonstration is complete. Let us stay here until a train stops.'

We didn't have long to wait. The very next train raced out of the tunnel as before, but slowed in the open. Then, with an ugly noise from brakes, it stopped immediately beneath us. It was a very short distance from the window to the roof of the train. Holmes softly closed the window.

'Our thinking has been correct so far,' he said. 'What do you reckon, Watson?'

'Amazing,' I said.

'There are still difficulties ahead,' said Holmes. 'But perhaps we may find something here to help us.'

We went up the back stairs and entered a group of rooms on the first floor. One was a dining room, containing nothing of interest. The second was a bedroom, also of no interest. The remaining room appeared more promising, and my friend started a careful search of it. But at the end of an hour he was no further forward.

'The clever old dog has cleaned up after himself,' he said. 'Any dangerous papers have been destroyed or removed. This box is our last chance.'

It was a small metal box which stood on the writing-desk. Holmes forced it open with one of our tools. There were several rolls of paper inside, covered with figures and calculations. Words occurred from time to time, which could have suggested some possible connection to a submarine. Holmes threw all the papers impatiently to one side. There only remained an envelope with some small newspaper cuttings inside. He shook them out on the table, and at once I saw from the look on his face that his hopes had been raised.

'What's this, Watson? What's this?' he cried. 'Some messages in the advertisement pages of a newspaper. From the letters and the paper, it looks like the *Daily Telegraph*. No dates, but we can work out the order. This must be the first: *Hoped to hear sooner. Price agreed. Write fully to address given. Pierrot.*

'The next reads: *Too complicated to describe. Must have full report. Your stuff is ready when everything delivered. Pierrot.*

'Then comes: *Matter urgent. Agreement ends unless delivery completed. Make appointment by letter. Check for my advertisement. Pierrot.*

'Finally: *Monday night after nine. Two taps. Only ourselves. Do not be so suspicious. Payment in cash when everything delivered. Pierrot.*'

'A fairly complete record, Watson! If only we could catch the man at the other end!' He sat lost in thought, tapping his fingers on the table. Finally he jumped to his feet.

'Well, perhaps it won't be so difficult, after all,' he said. 'There's nothing more we can do here, Watson. I think we might drive round to the offices of the *Daily Telegraph*, and so bring an end to a good day's work.'

* * *

Mycroft Holmes and Inspector Lestrade came round by appointment after breakfast the next day and Sherlock Holmes related what he and I had done the day before. The policeman shook his head over our confession of breaking into Oberstein's house.

'It's no surprise then that you get better results than we do,' he said. 'But one of these days you and your friend will find yourselves in trouble.'

'Ah! But we did it for England, and for home and for beauty, didn't we Watson?' grinned Holmes. 'We risked our freedom for our country. And what do you think of it, Mycroft?'

'Well done, Sherlock!' said Mycroft. 'Excellent! Truly excellent! But how can you make use of it?'

Holmes picked the *Daily Telegraph* up off the table.

'Have you seen Pierrot's advertisement today?' he asked.

'What? Another one?' said Mycroft.

'Yes, here it is,' said Holmes and read out:

Tonight. Same hour. Same place. Two taps. Most important. Your safety at risk. Pierrot.

'Good God!' cried Lestrade. 'If he answers that, we've got him!'

'That was my idea when I put it in the newspaper,' explained Holmes. 'If you could both come with us at about eight o'clock to Caulfield Gardens, we might possibly get a little nearer to a solution.'

One of the most remarkable features of Sherlock Holmes's character was his ability to switch all his thoughts onto lighter things once he had persuaded himself that there was no further work to be done. I remember that for the whole of that unforgettable day he lost himself in a study of Orlande Lassus, a musician from the Middle Ages. Of course, I have none of this ability to 'switch off'. For me, therefore, the day seemed never ending. I only began to relax a little when at last we set out from Baker Street.

Lestrade and Mycroft met us outside Gloucester Road Station. We had left the back door of Oberstein's house open the night before. By nine o'clock we were all sitting in the study, waiting patiently.

An hour passed and then another two. Lestrade and Mycroft moved nervously in their seats and kept looking at their watches. But Holmes sat silent and calm. His eyes were half shut, though every sense was very much awake. Suddenly he raised his head.

'He's coming,' he said.

There had been an almost silent step outside the door. Then another. Then two sharp taps on the door. Holmes rose, signalling us to remain sitting. There was hardly any light in the corridor. Holmes opened the front door. A dark figure moved quickly past him and Holmes closed and locked the door. 'This way!' we heard him say, and a moment later our man stood before us. Holmes had followed him closely. As the man turned with a cry of surprise and alarm, Holmes caught him by the collar and threw him back into the room. Before our prisoner had recovered his balance, the door was shut and Holmes stood with his back against it. The man looked angrily round. Then his eyes rolled up, and he fell unconscious to the floor. As he did so, his large hat flew off, the scarf fell from across his face, and there were the long light beard and the soft, handsome features of Colonel Valentine Walter.

Holmes gave a whistle of surprise.

'You can write me down as a fool this time, Watson,' he said. 'This was not the bird that I was looking for.'

'Who is he?' asked Mycroft excitedly.

'The younger brother of the late Sir James Walter, the head of the Submarine Department,' said Holmes.

Holmes put a finger to his lips.

'Ah!' he said. 'I see what's been happening here. I think that you had better let me question him.'

Our prisoner began to recover consciousness. He sat up and looked round, an expression of horror on his face.

'What's this?' he asked. 'I came here to visit Mr Oberstein.'

'We know everything, Colonel Walter,' said Holmes. 'We know everything about your relationship with Oberstein. We also know about the circumstances surrounding the death of young Cadogan West. An apology and a confession might make things a little easier for you, since there are still some details which only you can tell us about.'

The man groaned and put his face in his hands. We waited, but he was silent.

'Let me make it clear,' said Holmes, 'we know all the essential facts. We know you needed money. We know you made copies of your brother's keys. We know you started to deal with Oberstein, who answered your letters through advertisements in the *Daily Telegraph*. We know that you went to the Woolwich office on Monday night, but that you were seen and followed by young Cadogan West. It's likely that he had some previous reason to suspect you. He saw you steal the papers. However, he couldn't raise the alarm because it was just possible that you were taking the papers to your brother in London. Putting everything else to one side, like the faithful employee that he was, he followed you closely in the fog until you reached this house. Here he got involved. And it was here, Colonel Walter, that you added the terrible crime of murder to what you had already done.'

'I did not!' cried our sorry prisoner. 'I swear I did not!'

'Tell us, then,' said Holmes, 'what happened to Cadogan West before you put his body on the roof of the train.'

'I will. I swear to you,' answered the prisoner. 'I did the rest. I admit it. It was just as you say. I owed a large amount of money and Oberstein offered me five thousand pounds. But as for murder, I am innocent.'

'What happened, then?' asked Holmes.

'Cadogan West had had his suspicions before,' began Colonel Walter, 'and he followed me just as you described. I didn't realise it until I reached the front door. I'd given two taps and Oberstein had come to the door. The young man rushed up and demanded to know what we were about to do with the papers. Oberstein had a small metal cosh[12]. He always carried it with him. As West forced his way into the house, Oberstein hit him on the head and killed him. We had no idea what to do. Then Oberstein remembered that trains sometimes stopped under his back window. First he examined the papers I'd brought. He said that three of them were so technical that he must keep them. I didn't want him to, but he persuaded me that if we put the others into Cadogan West's pocket the young man would be blamed for the whole business. We waited for a train to stop at the window. Then we let West's body down onto the roof of the train.'

'And your brother?' asked Holmes.

'He said nothing,' replied Colonel Walter. 'But he'd caught me once before with his keys. I saw in his eyes that he suspected. As you know, it was the end for him.'

There was silence in the room. It was broken by Mycroft.

'Can you not make up for the damage you have done?' he suggested. 'It would make you feel better, and it might lessen your punishment.'

'How could I do that?' asked Colonel Walter.

'Didn't Oberstein leave you an address?' asked Mycroft.

'He said that letters to the Hotel du Louvre, Paris, would eventually reach him,' replied Colonel Walter.

'Then you are still able to help us,' said Sherlock Holmes.

'I'll do anything,' said Walter. 'This man has ruined me.'

'Here's some paper and a pen,' said Holmes. 'Sit at this desk and write down what I tell you:

Dear Sir, About the papers I gave you, you will no doubt have realised by now that one essential detail is missing. I have a copy of that detail which will make your information complete. I do not trust the post enough to send this to you. I would come to you abroad, but I am unable to leave the country at present. Therefore I shall expect to meet you in the lounge of the Charing Cross Hotel at noon on Saturday.

'That will do very well. I shall be very surprised if it does not catch our man.'

And it did! It's a matter of history – that secret history of a nation which is often so much more interesting than what is known publicly – that Oberstein could not turn down this golden opportunity. He came to collect the missing detail and was safely put away in a British prison for fifteen years. In his suitcase were the priceless Bruce-Partington plans, which he had been trying to sell to all the governments of Europe.

Colonel Walter died in prison towards the end of the second year of his sentence. As for Holmes, he returned enthusiastically to his study of Lassus and the music of the Middle Ages.

ACTIVITIES

1 Check your answers to *Before you read* on page 4.

2 Complete the summary of the story with the names in the box.

> Sherlock Holmes   Mycroft (x2)   Cadogan West
> Inspector Lestrade (x3)   Sir James Walter
> Colonel Valentine Walter (x2)   Violet Westbury
> Sidney Johnson   Watson (x4)   Hugo Oberstein (x3)

1 .... receives a telegram from his brother, 2 .... , about the death of a man called 3 .... and some missing papers. Mycroft and 4 .... visit Holmes and 5 .... in Baker Street to explain the case. Holmes, Watson and 6 .... go to Aldgate station, where Cadogan West's body was found. Then Holmes and 7 .... go to the house of 8 .... , but discover that he has died that morning. They speak to his brother, 9 .... After that, Holmes and Watson visit Cadogan West's mother and his fiancée, 10 .... Finally, Holmes and Watson visit 11 .... at his office in the Woolwich Arsenal. Holmes then continues his investigations alone. He later calls 12 .... and arranges to meet him at a restaurant in Kensington. That evening, Holmes and Watson break into the house of 13 .... , where they find a window overlooking the Underground line. Holmes puts a message in the newspaper, hoping Cadogan West's killer will see it. Holmes waits in 14 .... 's house with 15 .... , 16 .... and 17 .... for the thief and killer to arrive. After a while 18 .... arrives. He has stolen the papers, but 19 .... killed Cadogan West.

3 Put the events in order.

1 Oberstein takes three of the papers and puts the rest in Cadogan West's pocket. ☐

2 Cadogan West follows Colonel Walter to Oberstein's house. ☐

3 Cadogan West sees Colonel Walter near the Woolwich office and follows him. ☐

4 Cadogan West's body is found at Aldgate station. ☐

5 Cadogan West sees Colonel Walter take the submarine papers. ☐

6 Oberstein and Colonel Walter put Cadogan West's body onto the roof of a train. ☐

7 Oberstein hits Cadogan West on the head and kills him. ☐

4 How does Sherlock Holmes solve the case? Read the sentences and write T (true) or F (false) in the boxes.

1 Cadogan West did not have a train ticket. ☐

2 Cadogan West's body was thrown out of the window of a train. ☐

3 Sidney Johnson probably stole the plans to sell them. ☐

4 Cadogan West and Violet Westbury argued about something. ☐

5 Someone has broken the shutter of the window of the Woolwich Arsenal office. ☐

6 Some of the houses near the Underground line have windows above the train line. ☐

7 Cadogan West's body has been thrown out of the window of Oberstein's house. ☐

8 Oberstein is leaving secret messages in the newspaper, using the name 'Pierrot'. ☐

People in the story

Sherlock Holmes: the famous detective
Dr Watson: Sherlock Holmes's friend and assistant
Violet Hunter: a governess[13]
Miss Stoper: runs an employment agency
Jephro Rucastle: lives in the countryside near Winchester
Alice Rucastle: Jephro Rucastle's daughter by his first wife
Mrs Rucastle: Jephro Rucastle's second wife
Toller: Jephro Rucastle's servant
Mrs Toller: Toller's wife, also Jephro Rucastle's servant
Edward Rucastle: Jephro Rucastle's young son by his second wife
Mr Fowler: a friend of Alice Rucastle

BEFORE YOU READ
• •

1 What do you think the title refers to?

....

2 Look at the pictures on pages 47–73 and *People in the story* above. Who do you think the people are?

....

The Copper Beeches

'A person who loves any form of art,' said Sherlock Holmes, throwing his newspaper to one side, 'frequently gets the most pleasure from the simplest ideas. I'm happy to see, Watson, that you understand this. When you write your little records of my work, you have not emphasised my most dramatic cases. Instead, you've focused on those cases where the events seem almost unimportant, but which demonstrate my unmatched ability to use logic and clear thinking to solve a problem.'

I said nothing. Egotism[14] was one of the less attractive elements of my friend's unusual character.

It was a cold spring morning, and we sat on either side of a cheerful fire in the old room at Baker Street. Sherlock Holmes had been silent all morning, reading the newspapers. Then, having found nothing of interest, he had decided to pass on a few thoughts about my writing – some less positive criticism.

'I'm not being selfish or proud,' he continued. 'My art, the art of detection, is an impersonal thing – a thing beyond myself. Crime is common. Logic is rare. Therefore you should focus on the logic rather than on the crime. However, in putting colour and life into your work as a writer, you have turned what should have been a course of instruction into just a collection of stories.'

'Maybe,' I answered. 'However, I'd say that my account of your methods is original and interesting.'

'Good God!' replied Holmes. 'What do the public care about the finer points of investigation! The criminal classes have lost all their energy and originality. These days my work seems to involve little more than giving advice to young ladies about totally unimportant matters. And the note I had this morning marks a new low point, I suspect. Read it!' He threw a piece of paper across to me.

Dear Mr Holmes, I am very anxious to ask your advice about a job which has been offered to me as a governess. I shall call at half past ten. Yours faithfully, Violet Hunter

'It's half past ten now,' I said.

'Yes, and I have no doubt that is her at the door,' answered Holmes.

'It may turn out to be of more interest than you think,' I said. 'You've had other cases that appeared to be nothing at first, but later developed into serious investigations.'

'Well, let's hope so. Anyway, we shall soon find out.'

I went to open the door and welcome the young lady into the room. She was plainly but neatly dressed. She had a bright, quick face, and a lively manner.

'I'm sorry to trouble you,' she began, 'but I've had a very strange experience. And, as I have no parents or relations to ask for advice, I thought that you might be kind enough to help me.'

'Please take a seat, Miss Hunter,' said Holmes. 'I shall be happy to do whatever I can.'

I could see that Holmes was attracted by the manner and speech of his new client. He studied her in his usual searching way, and then sat back to listen to her story, with his eyes half closed.

'I've been a governess for five years,' she said, 'in the family of Colonel Spence Munro. However, two months ago the colonel moved to America, taking his children with him. I therefore found myself without a job. There is a well-known

agency for governesses in the West End called Westaway's and I've been calling in there from time to time in search of a new position. Well, when I called in last week, I found that Miss Stoper, the manager of the agency, was not alone. A hugely fat man with a smiling face and a great heavy chin was sitting next to her. He looked very keenly at me as I entered the room. In fact, he gave quite a jump in his chair and turned quickly to Miss Stoper. "She will do perfectly," he said. "I could not ask for anyone better." He seemed enthusiastic and friendly.

"You're looking for a position, miss?" he asked.

"Yes, sir," I replied.

"And what salary are you expecting?"

"I earned £4 a month in my last position."

"Oh dear!" he cried, throwing his fat hands into the air. "How terrible! How could anyone offer so little to such a fine and able young woman?"

"My abilities, sir, may be less than you imagine," I replied. "A little French, a little German, music, and drawing …"

"Well, your salary with me would start at £100 a year. I also like to pay my young ladies half their salary in advance," he said, smiling pleasantly. "In that way they can buy anything they need related to their journey, and the clothes they might need."

'You can imagine, Mr Holmes,' continued Miss Hunter, 'that such an offer seemed almost too good to be true. The gentleman, however, perhaps seeing disbelief in my face, opened his wallet and took out a note. It seemed to me that I had never met such a thoughtful man. I owed money to various people, so the advance would be extremely useful. However, there was something strange about the whole situation and I wanted to know more before I made any commitment. "May I ask where you live, sir?" I inquired of the man.

"Hampshire. A lovely house in the country called The Copper Beeches, five miles from Winchester," said the man. "In beautiful countryside."

"And my duties, sir?" I asked him.

"One dear little boy just six years old," he said. "Oh, if you could see him killing insects with a shoe! Smack! Smack! Smack! Three dead before you know it!" He leaned back in his chair and laughed. I was a little surprised by this comment, but his laughter made me think that perhaps he was joking.

"My only duty, then, is to look after a single child?"

"No, not just that, my dear young lady," he cried. "It would also be your duty to help my wife. Do you see any difficulty with that?"

"I'd be happy to make myself useful."

"Good," continued the man. "Take dress, for example. We are fussy people, you know – fussy, but kind-hearted. If we asked you to wear a particular dress that we might give you, would you object?"

"No," I answered, although I was rather surprised by this.

"Or to sit here, or sit there, that would not be a problem for you?"

"No."

"Or to cut your hair quite short before you come to us?"

"I'm afraid that is quite impossible," I replied. He was watching me keenly, and I saw a shadow pass over his face as I spoke.

"I'm afraid that is essential," he said. "It's a little whim[15] of my wife's. And I do like to try and satisfy her whims. So you won't cut your hair?"

"No, sir, I really couldn't," I answered firmly.

"Very well," he said. "Unfortunately that settles the matter. It is a pity, because you really would have been very suitable. In that case, Miss Stoper, I'd better see a few more of your young ladies."

Miss Hunter looked at me, then back at Holmes.

'I could hardly believe my ears,' she said. 'As you can see, Mr Holmes, my hair is thick and attractive, and a rather unusual shade of chestnut[16]. I wouldn't dream of cutting it off for so little reason.

'Well,' she continued, 'when I got back to my rooms, I began to wonder if I'd been very foolish. Few governesses in England earn £100 a year. Besides, what use was my hair to me? Many people look better with short hair. Maybe I was one of them. After a few days I decided I'd made a mistake. In fact, I was about to go back to the agency and inquire whether the position was still open, when I received this letter. I'll read it to you:

The Copper Beeches, near Winchester

Dear Miss Hunter

Miss Stoper has kindly given me your address, and I am writing to ask you whether you have reconsidered your decision. I have told my wife about you and she is very anxious that you should come. We are willing to pay £120 a year to reward you for any inconvenience which our requests may cause. My wife is fond of a particular shade of electric blue and would like you to wear a blue dress indoors in the morning. You do not need to buy one, however. We have one belonging to my dear daughter Alice (who is now in Philadelphia), which would, I think, fit you very well. Then, we may ask you to sit here or there, or to amuse yourself in a particular way, but this need not cause you any inconvenience. As for your hair, I am afraid I must remain firm on this point. I only hope that the increased salary will make up for the loss. Your duties, as far as the child is concerned, are very light. Please do try to come.

Yours sincerely,

Jephro Rucastle

'I've decided that I will accept the position,' continued Miss Hunter. 'However, I thought that before taking the final step I'd ask your advice.'

'Well, Miss Hunter, if you've decided, that settles the question,' said Holmes, smiling.

'But you wouldn't advise me to refuse?'

'It's not a situation which I'd like to see a sister of mine apply for,' replied Holmes.

'But, Mr Holmes, what does it all mean?'

'I have no facts,' replied Holmes. 'I cannot say. Perhaps you have an opinion?'

'Well, there seems to be only one possible solution,' said Miss Hunter. Mr Rucastle seemed a very kind, friendly man. Presumably his wife is mad. He wants to keep the matter quiet because he's afraid she might get taken away to a mental hospital. And that's why he allows her these whims.'

'That's possible,' agreed Holmes. 'In fact, it's the most probable explanation. Nevertheless, it doesn't seem a nice situation for a young lady.'

'But the money, Mr Holmes!'

'Well, yes, of course the pay is good. But too good. That's what worries me. Why should they give you £120 a year, when they could easily find someone for £40? There must be a reason.'

'I thought that if I told you the circumstances now you would understand if I later wanted your help,' said Miss Hunter. 'I'd feel so much stronger if I knew that I could depend on your support.'

'Oh, you may certainly depend on that,' said Holmes. 'Your little problem promises to be most interesting. If you find yourself in doubt or in danger ...'

'Danger! What danger do you expect?'

Holmes shook his head, a serious expression on his face. 'It wouldn't be a danger if we knew what it was. But at any time, day or night, I'm ready to come to your aid.'

'Thank you.' Miss Hunter got up quickly from her chair, the worry gone from her face. 'I shall write to Mr Rucastle at once, cut my poor hair, and start for Winchester tomorrow.'

With a few more grateful words, she said goodbye and went on her way.

'At least,' I said as she went off down the street, 'she seems well able to take care of herself.'

'She needs to be,' said Holmes. 'I'll be very surprised if we don't hear from her before long.'

It turned out that Holmes was right. A fortnight went past. Then late one night we heard from Miss Hunter. The message was brief and urgent.

Please be at the Black Swan Hotel in Winchester at midday tomorrow. Do come! I don't know what to do.
Violet Hunter

By eleven o'clock the next day we were well on our way to Winchester. As we passed into Hampshire, Holmes threw down his newspaper and began to enjoy the scenery. It was a beautiful spring day. There were rolling hills, red farmhouse roofs, bright sunshine and the light green of the new season's leaves.

'Is this not beautiful?' I cried enthusiastically, a man fresh from the dirt of the city.

But Holmes just shook his head.

'Watson,' he said, 'you look at these houses and hills and see their beauty. I see only how easy it would be to commit a crime and escape punishment.'

'What on earth do you mean?' I asked.

'In town,' replied Holmes, 'public opinion can do what the law cannot. If people hear the scream of a child or the sound of a punch, they can take appropriate action. One word of complaint will bring the police, and there is little distance between the crime and the court.'

Holmes pointed out of the window.

'Look at these lonely houses. Think of the terrible crimes which may go on in such places, and nobody knows anything about them. If Miss Hunter had gone to live in Winchester, I'd have had no fear for her. But she's five miles out in the countryside. That's where the danger is. Still, it's clear that she's not personally threatened.'

'No. If she can come to Winchester to meet us, she can get away,' I said. 'But what *can* be the matter?'

'I've thought of seven separate explanations,' said Holmes. 'But which of them is correct will depend on fresh information.'

The Black Swan is a well-known hotel in the High Street, not far from the station, and there we found the young lady waiting for us.

'I'm so glad that you've come,' she said. 'I just don't know what to do.'

'Tell us what's happened,' I said.

'I will, but I must be quick. I've promised Mr Rucastle to be back before three as he and Mrs Rucastle are going out tonight. I got his permission to come into town this morning, although he doesn't know why.'

'Tell us everything in order,' said Holmes, stretching his legs out towards the fire.

'Firstly,' began Miss Hunter, 'I have to say that I have not been treated badly at all by Mr and Mrs Rucastle. But I cannot understand them. And that worries me.'

'What can't you understand?' asked Holmes.

'The reasons for what they do and what they ask me to do. But let me tell you everything. The Copper Beeches is indeed beautifully situated, but it isn't a beautiful house – just a large square building. There are woods on three sides, and on the fourth there is a field which goes down to the main road. This is about a hundred metres from the front door. There's a group of copper beech trees just near the front door, which explains the name of the house.

'My employer, who was as friendly as ever, drove me to the house and that evening he introduced me to his wife and child. There was no truth, Mr Holmes, in our previous discussion. Mrs Rucastle is not mad. She's silent, pale-faced, and much younger than her husband. I understand they've been married for about seven years. He was a widower. And his only child by his first wife is the daughter, Alice, who has gone to Philadelphia. In private, Mr Rucastle told me that she'd left because she strongly disliked her stepmother, his new wife. Since the daughter must be over twenty, I can imagine that she might have felt uncomfortable with her father's young wife.'

Miss Hunter moved a little on her chair and continued.

'To me Mrs Rucastle seems colourless in mind as well as in appearance,' she said. 'I have no strong feelings about her, positive or negative. She is clearly extremely fond of both her husband and her little son. And yet she has some secret sadness. More than once I have found her in tears. I felt sometimes it might be her son's behaviour that worried her. He's full of anger and his main enjoyment seems to be catching and harming small animals. But that has little to do with my story.'

'I'm glad of all details,' commented my friend, 'whether they seem important or not.'

'The one unpleasant thing about the house,' continued Miss Hunter, 'is the servants. There are two, a man and his wife. The man is called Toller. He's a rough, rude man, with untidy hair and a beard. His wife is a tall woman with an unpleasant face. She's as silent as Mrs Rucastle and much less friendly.

'For the first two days my life was very quiet. On the third, Mrs Rucastle came down just after breakfast and whispered something to her husband. "Oh, yes," he said, turning to me, "we'd like to thank you very much, Miss Hunter, for agreeing to cut your hair. It certainly hasn't taken away from your appearance in any way at all. And we'd now like to see how the electric blue dress suits you. You'll find it on the bed in your room."

'The dress was a peculiar shade of blue. It was of excellent material, and it had obviously been worn before. Nevertheless, it was a perfect fit. Both Mr and Mrs Rucastle were delighted at how I looked, in fact rather over-delighted. They were waiting for me in the sitting room. A chair had been placed close to the central window in this room, with its back towards the window. I was asked to sit in the chair, and then Mr Rucastle began to tell me the most amusing stories.

'You cannot imagine how funny he was. I laughed until I was almost exhausted. Mrs Rucastle, however, just sat with her hands together, and an anxious look on her face. After an hour or so, Mr Rucastle suddenly stopped and asked me to change my dress and go and look after little Edward.

'Two days later we went through exactly the same performance. Again I changed my dress, again I sat in the window, and again I laughed and laughed at the funny stories. Then Mr Rucastle handed me a book and asked me to read to him. I read for about ten minutes, and then suddenly, in the middle of a sentence, he ordered me to stop and to change my dress.

'They were always careful to turn my face away from the window. And so, I decided I needed to see what was happening behind my back. I have a small mirror that's broken, so I hid a piece of the glass in my handkerchief. On the next occasion, in the middle of my laughter, I put my handkerchief up to my eyes, and was able to see everything that was behind me. I noticed that there was a man standing on the main road, looking in my direction. When I put down my handkerchief, Mrs Rucastle's eyes were fixed on me in a most searching manner. I'm sure she realised that I had a mirror in my hand. She stood up at once. "Jephro," she said, "there's a rude man on the road down there staring at Miss Hunter."

"A friend of yours, Miss Hunter?" he asked.

"No, I know no one in this part of the world."

"Dear me! How very rude! Please turn round and wave him away."

"Surely it would be better to take no notice," I suggested.

"No, no. He'll be standing around here all the time otherwise. Please wave him away."

'I did as I was told, and then immediately Mrs Rucastle

closed the curtains. That was a week ago, and since then I have not sat in the window, nor worn the blue dress, nor seen the man in the road.'

'Most interesting,' said Holmes. 'Please continue.'

'The rest is rather mixed up I'm afraid,' said Miss Hunter. 'On the very first day that I was at the Copper Beeches, Mr Rucastle took me to a small wooden hut near the kitchen door. As we approached, I heard a sound like a large animal moving about. "Look in here!" said Mr Rucastle, showing me a hole in the door. "Isn't he a beauty?"

'I looked through the hole and was conscious of two fierce eyes, and of a large figure in the darkness.

"Don't be frightened," said my employer, laughing when I jumped backwards. "It's only Carlo, my guard dog. Toller feeds him once a day, but not too much, so he's always ready for action. Toller lets him loose every night, and God help anyone he gets his teeth into. Don't ever leave the house at night for any reason. It would be most dangerous."

'The warning was quite serious and sent an icy feeling down my back. And then I had another strange experience. As you know, I cut off my hair in London. However, I kept it – in the bottom of my suitcase. One evening, I began to rearrange things in my room. There's an old chest of drawers there, the two upper drawers empty and open, the lower one locked. I wondered if the third drawer might have been locked by mistake, so I took out my keys and tried to open it. The very first key fitted perfectly and opened the drawer. There was just one thing in it – my hair!

'I picked it up and examined it. It was of the same unusual colour, and the same thickness. But how could my hair have become locked in the drawer? With shaking hands I undid my suitcase, looked in the bottom and found my own hair. I laid the two lots of hair next to each other and they were exactly the same. Isn't that extraordinary? I just couldn't understand it. I put the strange hair back, and said nothing about it.

'As you may have noticed, Mr Holmes, I'm naturally observant, and I soon had a good plan of the whole house in my head. There was one side, however, which appeared not to be used. I found the door to this part of the house, but it was always locked. One day I met Mr Rucastle coming out of this door. He appeared a very different person to the round, cheerful man I was used to. His cheeks were red and his forehead was lined with anger. He locked the door and hurried past me without a word or a look.

'This made me curious, so when I went out for a walk, I wandered round to this side of the house. Upstairs there were four windows in a row, three of which were simply dirty, while the fourth had the curtains closed. They were obviously all empty. As I walked up and down, Mr Rucastle came out of the house, looking as cheerful as ever. "Ah!" he said. "You mustn't think that I was being rude just now, my dear young lady. I was very worried about some business matters." I told him he hadn't been rude at all.

"By the way," I said to Mr Rucastle, "you seem to have quite a few spare rooms up there, and one of them has the curtains closed." He looked surprised at my comment.

"Photography is one of my hobbies," he replied. "I have a dark room up there. What an observant young lady you are!" He said this jokingly, but there was no laughter in his eyes. I saw only suspicion and annoyance.

'Well, Mr Holmes, from the moment that I realised there was something secret about those rooms, I was desperate to get into them. It wasn't just curiosity. It was more a feeling of duty – a feeling that some good might come from my getting in there.

'Yesterday the chance came. As well as Mr Rucastle, both Toller and his wife go into these empty rooms. Yesterday Toller was very unwell, and when I went upstairs the key was still in the door. Doubtless he'd left it there by mistake. Mr and Mrs Rucastle were both downstairs, and the child was with them. It was a fantastic opportunity. I quietly opened the door and went through.

'There was a small dark corridor and three doors in a line. The first and third were open. They each led into an empty room. The middle door was closed, and across the outside was an iron bar, locked at one end to a ring in the wall, and tied at the other with thick rope. The door itself was locked as well, and the key was not there. This door clearly led to the room with the closed curtains, and yet I could see from the light beneath the door that the room was not dark inside. There must be a skylight[17] which let in light from above. Suddenly I heard footsteps inside the room and a shadow passed across the light. It terrified me, Mr Holmes. I felt frightened for my life. I turned and ran – down the corridor, through the door, and straight into the arms of Mr Rucastle.

"So," he said, smiling, "it was you, then. I thought it must be when I saw the door open."

"Oh, I'm so frightened!" I gasped.

"My dear young lady! What has frightened you?"

'You cannot imagine how caring and gentle his manner was. But his voice was just a little too sweet. I immediately became careful with my words.

"I was foolish enough to go in there," I answered him. "But it's so ghostly I became frightened and ran out again. Oh, it's so awfully still in there!"

"Why do you think that I lock the door?"

"I've no idea."

"It's to keep people out who have no business there. Do you understand?" He was still smiling in the most friendly manner.

"I'm sure if I'd known ..." I began.

"Well, you know now," he interrupted. "And if you ever set foot in there again ..." Here the smile hardened into a furious grin "... I'll throw you to the dog."

'I was so terrified that I don't know what I did. I must have rushed to my room. I remember nothing until I found myself lying on my bed shaking all over. Then I thought of you, Mr Holmes. I could not live there any longer without some advice. Of course, I might have just run away, but I was as curious as I was afraid. If I could only persuade you to come, everything would be all right. Now I have told you all my adventures, Mr Holmes. Perhaps you could tell me what's going on and what I should do.'

Holmes and I had listened with complete attention to this extraordinary story. There was a most serious expression on Holmes's face.

'Is Toller still unwell?' he asked.

'Yes,' replied Miss Hunter. 'I heard his wife tell Mrs Rucastle that he was hardly able to do anything.'

'That is helpful,' said Holmes. 'And the Rucastles go out tonight?'

'Yes.'

'Is there a cellar[18] with a good strong lock?' asked Holmes.

'Yes, they keep wine there,' replied Miss Hunter.

'Throughout this affair you seem to have acted very bravely and sensibly, Miss Hunter,' said Holmes. 'Do you think that you could do one more thing? I wouldn't ask if I didn't think you a quite remarkable woman.'

'I'll try,' answered Miss Hunter. 'What is it?'

'My friend and I will be at the Copper Beeches by seven o'clock tonight,' explained Holmes. 'The Rucastles will be gone by then, and Toller will, we hope, still be too ill to do anything. There only remains Mrs Toller. If you could find some reason to send her into the cellar, and then lock her in, you'd make matters much easier.'

'I can do that,' said Miss Hunter.

'Excellent!' said Holmes. 'We will investigate the matter thoroughly. Of course, there's only one possible explanation. The Rucastles have brought you to their house to pretend to be someone. And the person you are pretending to be is a prisoner in that room. That's obvious. Who is the prisoner? I've no doubt that it's the daughter, Miss Alice Rucastle, who was said to have gone to America. You were chosen, doubtless, because you are similar to her in height, figure, and the colour of your hair. Hers was cut short, perhaps because of an illness. So, of course, yours had to be cut short too. By a curious chance you found her hair. The man in the road was, I am sure, a friend of hers – possibly the man she wants to marry. And no doubt the idea was to make him think you were Alice. He would believe from your laughter, and later when you waved him away, that you were no longer interested in him. The dog is let loose at night to prevent him from trying to communicate with her. All that is fairly clear. The most serious point in the case is the behaviour of the young boy.'

'What on earth has that got to do with it?' I asked.

'My dear Watson, as a doctor, you continually look for information about a child by studying the parents. Don't you see that the opposite is equally true. I have frequently got my first real understanding of the character of parents by studying their children. This child's behaviour is unnaturally cruel. I don't know whether he gets this from his smiling father, as I would suspect, or from his mother. However, things do not look good for poor Alice if she is in their power.'

'I'm sure that you are right, Mr Holmes,' cried Miss Hunter. 'We must help this poor woman.'

'We must also be careful,' warned Holmes. 'We're dealing with a very clever man. But we can do nothing until seven o'clock. Then we'll join you and solve the mystery.'

It was just seven when Holmes and I reached the Copper Beeches. The group of trees, with their dark leaves shining like metal in the light of the setting sun, were enough to let us know we were at the right house. Miss Hunter was standing on the doorstep.

'Have you managed it?' asked Holmes.

A loud noise came from somewhere downstairs. 'That's Mrs Toller in the cellar,' Miss Hunter said. 'Her husband is snoring in an armchair in the kitchen. Here are his keys.'

'You've done very well!' cried Holmes enthusiastically. 'Now lead the way.'

We climbed the stairs and found the door which Miss Hunter had described. Holmes cut the rope and removed the iron bar. Then he tried the various keys in the lock, but without success. No sound came from within, and Holmes's face grew dark at the silence.

'I hope we're not too late,' he said. 'Come on, Watson, put your shoulder to it. Let's break our way in.'

It was an old door and opened at once. Together we rushed into the room. It was empty. There was no furniture except a small bed and a table. The skylight above was open, and the prisoner gone.

'This is not good,' said Holmes. 'Someone has guessed our intentions and taken her away.'

'But how?'

'Through the skylight.' Holmes looked out onto the roof. 'Ah, yes,' he cried, 'there's a long ladder[19] against the side of the house.'

'But that's impossible,' said Miss Hunter. 'The ladder wasn't there when the Rucastles left.'

'Mr Rucastle must have come back,' said Holmes. 'I tell you he's a clever and dangerous man. I expect this is him I can hear now on the stairs. Watson, you should have your pistol ready.'

The words were hardly out of his mouth before a very fat man appeared, with a heavy stick in his hand. At the sight of him Miss Hunter screamed and moved back against the wall, but Holmes jumped forward in front of him.

'You evil man!' he said. 'Where's your daughter?'

The fat man looked around, and then up at the open skylight.

'It's for me to ask you that,' he shouted. 'You thieves! I've caught you now. You'll pay for this!' He turned and ran down the stairs as fast as he could go.

'He's gone for the dog!' cried Miss Hunter.

'We should close the front door,' cried Holmes, and we all rushed down the stairs together. We had hardly reached the hall when we heard the noise of the dog, and then a scream of pain. An old man with a red face, presumably Toller, came shakily out of a side door.

'My God!' he cried. 'Someone has let loose the dog. It hasn't been fed for two days. Quick, quick, or it'll be too late!'

Holmes and I rushed outside and round the corner of the house, with Toller behind us. There was the huge hungry animal, its black face buried in Rucastle's throat, while he lay on the ground screaming.

Running up, I shot the dog in the head, and it fell over with its sharp teeth still stuck in the fat man's neck. With great effort we separated them and carried the man, alive but horribly injured, into the house. We laid him on the sitting room sofa, and sent Toller to take the news to Rucastle's wife. I then did what I could to help the injured man. We were all gathered round him when the door opened, and a tall woman entered the room.

'Mrs Toller!' cried Miss Hunter.

'Mr Rucastle let me out of the cellar when he came back. It is a pity you didn't tell me what you were planning. I could have told you that your efforts would be wasted.'

'Ah!' said Holmes, looking keenly at her. 'It's clear that Mrs Toller knows more about this than anyone else.'

'Yes, sir, I do.'

'Then, please sit down,' said Holmes, 'and tell us. I must admit there are several points about which I am still unclear.'

'I'll explain everything,' said Mrs Toller. 'If this case goes to court, you'll remember that I never did you any harm, miss, and that I was Miss Alice's friend.'

Mrs Toller looked round at everyone.

'Miss Alice was never happy at home,' she began. 'Not since her father married again. But things only became really bad for her when she met Mr Fowler at a friend's house. As far as I could discover, Miss Alice had money of her own from her mother's will[20], but she was so quiet and patient she just left everything in Mr Rucastle's hands. He knew he was safe while she was on her own. But then, when there was a chance of a husband, who might ask for everything that was hers by law, her father thought it was time to put a stop to it. He wanted her to sign a paper, so that whether she married or not, he could still use her money. She wouldn't do it.

'But he kept on at her about it until she became stressed and ill. For six weeks we thought she would die, she was so out of her mind. That's when she cut off her hair. But eventually she got better. Still, she was just a shadow of herself, and without her beautiful hair. However, her young man stuck to her like a true man does.'

'Ah,' said Holmes, 'Mr Rucastle then decided to keep her a prisoner in the house?'

'Yes, sir.'

'And he brought Miss Hunter down here from London in order to get rid of the "annoying" Mr Fowler.'

'Exactly, sir.'

'But Mr Fowler, being a determined man,' continued Holmes, 'found out where she was. And he persuaded you by the strength of his arguments or maybe the openness of his wallet that you might be willing to help him.'

'Mr Fowler was a very kind, generous gentleman,' said Mrs Toller without a smile.

'And in this way he organised that a ladder would be ready just when Mr Rucastle had gone out.'

'Exactly.'

'Thank you, Mrs Toller,' said Holmes. 'You have certainly cleared everything up. And here comes the local doctor and Mrs Rucastle. I think, Watson, that we should take Miss Hunter back to Winchester. It seems to me that our reasons for being here are rather questionable.'

And that's how the strange mystery of the house with the copper beeches was solved. Mr Rucastle lived, but was always a broken man. He was only kept alive by the care of his loving wife. The Tollers still live with them. Mr Fowler and Miss Rucastle were married in Southampton the day after their escape. And they now live on the island of Mauritius. As for Miss Violet Hunter, my friend Holmes, rather to my disappointment, showed no further interest in her once she had stopped being the centre of one of his problems. She is now the head of a private school in Walsall, where she has been extremely successful.

ACTIVITIES

1 Check your answers to *Before you read* on page 46.

2 Put the sentences from Miss Hunter's diary in order.

1 I cut my hair. ☐
2 I found some hair exactly like mine in my bedroom. ☐
3 I went to an agency looking for a new job as a governess. ☐
4 I had to wear a blue dress and sit near the window. ☐
5 Mr Rucastle asked me to cut my hair short and I refused. ☐
6 I asked Sherlock Holmes to meet me in Winchester. ☐
7 I met a man called Mr Rucastle, who wanted a governess for his young son. ☐
8 I wrote to Mr Rucastle accepting the job as governess. ☐
9 I saw a man in the garden with my mirror. ☐
10 I started work at the Copper Beeches. ☐

3 Who or what do the <u>underlined</u> words refer to in these sentences from the story?

1 <u>He's</u> full of anger and his main enjoyment seems to be catching and harming small animals. ....
2 <u>It</u> was of excellent material and it had obviously been worn before. ....
3 Please turn around and wave <u>him</u> away. ....
4 Toller lets <u>him</u> loose every night and God help anyone he gets his teeth into. ....
5 I kept <u>it</u> – in the bottom of my suitcase. ....
6 If you could find some reason to send <u>her</u> into the cellar, and lock her in ... .
7 For six weeks we thought <u>she</u> would die, she was so out of her mind. ....
8 Running up, <u>I</u> shot the dog in the head. ....

74

4 What happened to Alice Rucastle? Match the two parts of the sentences.

1 When Alice's mother died ☐
2 After Alice's mother died ☐
3 When Alice met Mr Fowler ☐
4 When Mr Rucastle asked to use Alice's money ☐
5 When Alice became ill ☐
6 When Alice was locked in a room ☐
7 After Alice climbed through the skylight ☐
8 After Alice and Mr Fowler were married ☐

a she refused.
b they went to Mauritius.
c she left Alice some money.
d she fell in love.
e Mr Rucastle said she had gone to America
f her father married again.
g she escaped down the ladder.
h she cut her hair.

5 Answer the questions.

1 Why does Miss Hunter go to visit Sherlock Holmes the first time?

2 Why does Mr Rucastle want Miss Hunter to work for his family?

3 Why does Miss Hunter go up to the secret rooms?

4 After Miss Hunter goes to work at the Copper Beeches, why does she write to Holmes?

5 Why does Mrs Toller help Mr Fowler rescue Alice?

People in the story

Sherlock Holmes: the famous detective
Dr Watson: Sherlock Holmes's friend and assistant
Mr Roundhay: a vicar[21]
Mortimer Tregennis: a lodger at the vicar's house
Owen and George Tregennis: Mortimer's brothers
Brenda Tregennis: Mortimer's sister
Mrs Porter: cook and housekeeper for Owen, George and
    Brenda
Dr Leon Sterndale: a lion hunter and explorer

BEFORE YOU READ

1 Where do you think the story takes place?

2 Look at the pictures on pages 77–107 and *People in the story* above. Who do you think the people are?

The Devil's Foot

My long friendship with Mr Sherlock Holmes has led to many interesting experiences. However, when recording these adventures, I've often been faced with the difficulties caused by Holmes's hatred of publicity. In fact, he enjoys nothing more at the end of a successful case than to hand over the actual arrest to the police. He will then listen with an amused smile to all the misplaced congratulation. Indeed it's this attitude, rather than any absence of interesting material, which has caused me to write up so few of his recent cases.

It was, therefore, with considerable surprise that I received the following message from Holmes last Tuesday:

Why not write about the Cornish horror? The strangest case I have investigated.

I hurriedly searched for my notes so that I could write up the story.

In the spring of 1897 Holmes's normally excellent health was being damaged by continual hard work. Eventually Dr Moore Agar, a Harley Street specialist, gave clear instructions that the famous detective should stop work on all his cases and allow himself some weeks of complete rest. Otherwise, Dr Agar felt, it would be impossible to avoid a complete breakdown. Holmes, of course, never took the faintest interest in his health. However, under the threat that he might never again be able to work, he was eventually persuaded to give himself a complete change of scene and air. As a result, we found ourselves together in early spring in a small cottage near Poldhu Bay, at the furthest end of Cornwall[22].

It was an unusual spot, and peculiarly well suited to the dark mood of my friend. Our little white-painted house stood high on a grassy hill. From the windows we looked down on the evil-looking half-moon shape of Mounts Bay. Bordered by steep black cliffs[23] and with dangerous rocks hiding just beneath the water, the bay is a death trap for ships. Sensible sailors stay well away.

On land our surroundings were cheerless too. It was wild, treeless countryside, lonely, and with a remarkable absence of green. An occasional church tower marked the site of some old-world village. In every direction there were signs of an earlier type of people: strange monuments of stone, indications of prehistoric 'castles'. The evil mystery of the place attracted Holmes's imagination, and he went for many long walks on his own across the countryside.

The ancient Cornish language had also caught his attention. In order to develop his ideas, he'd sent for some books about the language. However, it would be some time before he could make a start on his studies. Even in that land of dreams, we found ourselves thrown into a problem that was deeper and more mysterious than anything we'd left behind in London. Holmes could not hide his delight; but, since I was looking after him, I was less happy when our peaceful, healthy routine was violently interrupted.

The nearest village was a tiny place called Tredannick Wollas, where cottages gather round an ancient church. The local vicar, Mr Roundhay, was interested in archaeology. Because of this, Holmes had got to know him. Roundhay was a middle-aged man, overweight and chatty, with considerable local knowledge. At his invitation we'd gone to his house, the vicarage, for tea, where we'd also got to know Mr Mortimer Tregennis. Tregennis lived in Roundhay's large house, paying him rent for the use of a couple of rooms. Tregennis was a thin dark man. He seemed bent, as if his body was in some way deformed. I remember that during our short visit we found the vicar very chatty, but his lodger[24] strangely silent. He was sad-faced, and sat looking away from us, apparently thinking about his own affairs.

These were the two men who suddenly entered our sitting

room on Tuesday, March the 16th, soon after breakfast. Holmes and I were sitting and chatting, just before setting off for our daily walk.

'Mr Holmes,' said the vicar in an anxious voice, 'the most awful thing has occurred during the night. We can only think ourselves incredibly lucky that you should be here at this time.'

I stared rather angrily at the vicar, for he was disturbing our rest and relaxation; but Holmes sat up in his chair like an old hunting dog that suddenly catches the smell of a fox. He waved his hand at the sofa and our anxious visitors sat down side by side. They obviously shared a common concern.

'Shall I speak or you?' Tregennis asked the vicar.

'Well, you seem to have made the discovery, whatever it may be,' said Holmes. 'And the vicar only knows about it second-hand. So perhaps you had better do the speaking,' said Holmes to Tregennis.

I was amused to see how surprised they were that Holmes knew this. However, his logic was simple. The vicar had obviously dressed in a hurry, whereas the lodger, sitting beside him, was more formally dressed.

'Perhaps I'd better say a few words first,' said the vicar. 'Mr Tregennis spent yesterday evening with his two brothers, Owen and George, and his sister Brenda, at their house in the village of Tredannick Wartha. When he left them, soon after ten o'clock, they were playing cards round the dining room table, in excellent health and very good humour. This morning, being an early riser, he walked in that direction before breakfast. On the way he was overtaken by Dr Richards, who explained that he had just been called urgently to the Tregennis household in Tredannick Wartha. Mr Mortimer Tregennis naturally went along with him.

'When they arrived they found an extraordinary situation. Mr Tregennis's two brothers and his sister were seated round the table exactly as he had left them. Their cards were still spread in front of them. And the candles[25] had completely burned down. His sister was lying back in her chair, stone-dead. His two brothers were sitting on each side of her talking nonsense, shouting, and singing. They had totally lost their senses. All three of them, the dead woman and the two crazy men, had on their faces an expression of complete horror, terror even. There was no sign that anyone had been in the house, except Mrs Porter, the old cook and housekeeper. She said that she had slept deeply and heard no sound during the night. Nothing was out of place or had been stolen. And there's absolutely no explanation of what the horror can be that has frightened a woman to death and two strong men out of their senses. In brief, Mr Holmes, that's the situation. If you can help us to clear it up, you'll have done an excellent piece of work.'

Somehow I had hoped that I might persuade my friend to continue his healthy routine of rest and quiet. However, one look at the concentration on his face told me how little chance I had. He sat for some time in silence.

'I'll look into it,' Holmes said at last. 'At first sight, it would appear to be an extraordinary case. Have you been there yourself, Mr Roundhay?'

'No, Mr Holmes,' replied Roundhay. 'Mr Tregennis came back to the house and told me. We immediately hurried here to find you.'

'How far is it to the house where this awful event occurred?' asked Holmes.

'About fifteen minutes' walk,' replied Roundhay.

'Then we shall go there together,' said Holmes. 'But first I must ask you a few questions, Mr Tregennis.'

Tregennis had been silent all this time, but I had noticed that he was as shaken as the vicar. His face was pale. His lips moved uncontrollably. And the look in his dark eyes seemed to suggest something of the horror of the scene.

'Ask what you like, Mr Holmes,' said Tregennis keenly. 'It's a horrible thing to talk about, but I will tell you the truth.'

'Tell me about the evening,' said Holmes.

'Well, Mr Holmes,' began Tregennis. 'I had a meal there, as the vicar has said. Afterwards my brother George suggested a game of cards. That was at about nine o'clock. It was a quarter past ten when I left. They were all round the table, as happy as could be.'

'Who let you out?' asked Holmes.

'I let myself out,' replied Tregennis. 'I shut the hall door behind me. The window of the room where they were was shut, but the curtains weren't closed. This morning the door and the window were exactly as I'd left them. And there was no reason to think anyone else had been to the house. Yet, I found them there, mad with terror, and Brenda dead. I'll never get that sight out of my mind as long as I live.'

'The facts, as you tell them, are certainly most remarkable,' said Holmes. 'I take it that you have no ideas yourself that might explain what happened?'

'It's evil, Mr Holmes,' cried Mortimer Tregennis. 'It is the work of the devil[26]! It is not of this world. How could it in any way be the result of something human?'

'I fear,' said Holmes, 'that if the matter is beyond human explanation, it's certainly beyond me. Yet we must examine all possible natural solutions before we consider an idea like that. As for you, Mr Tregennis, I take it you must have disagreed or argued with your family in some way, since they lived together and you had rooms with Mr Roundhay?'

'Yes, Mr Holmes,' answered Tregennis. 'However, that's all in the past now. We had a family business, which we sold, and we were able to retire with enough money to live on. I won't deny that there was some disagreement about the division of the money. And for a time it was a problem between us. But later it was all forgiven and forgotten, and we became the best of friends again.'

'Looking back at yesterday evening,' said Holmes, 'do you remember anything that might throw light on this awful situation? Think carefully, Mr Tregennis, for any clue which might help me.'

'There's nothing at all, sir,' replied Tregennis.

'Your family were behaving perfectly normally?' asked Holmes.

'Absolutely,' replied Tregennis.

'Did they show any concern about some kind of approaching danger?' asked Holmes.

'No,' replied Tregennis. 'Nothing like that at all.'

'You have nothing to add then, which could help me?'

Mortimer Tregennis thought carefully for a moment.

'There is one thing,' he said at last. 'As we sat at the table my back was to the window, and my brother George was sitting opposite me, facing it. I saw him once look hard over my shoulder, so I turned round and looked also. I could just see the bushes outside. I thought for a moment that I saw something moving among them. I couldn't even say if it was man or animal. But I just thought there was something there. When I asked him what he was looking at, he told me he had the same feeling. That's all I can say.'

'Didn't you investigate?' asked Holmes.

'It didn't seem important at the time,' replied Tregennis.

'You left them, then, without any feeling that there was something evil close by?' said Holmes.

'I had no feeling like that at all,' replied Tregennis.

'Tell me about the scene at the house this morning,' said Holmes.

'When the doctor and I arrived, we immediately entered that awful room,' said Tregennis. 'The candles and the fire must have burned out hours before, and they had been sitting there in the dark until dawn had come. The doctor said Brenda must have been dead for at least six hours. There were no signs of violence. She just lay in the chair with that look of terror on her face. George and Owen were singing lines from songs and making ridiculous noises like two great apes. Oh, it was awful to see! The doctor was as white as a sheet. In fact, he fell into a chair in a sort of faint. We nearly had him to look after as well.'

'Remarkable!' said Holmes, standing up and reaching for his hat. 'We had better go to Tredannick Wartha without further delay. I've rarely come across a more unusual problem.'

Our actions that first morning did little to take the investigation forwards. There was, however, an event which left me feeling most disturbed. While we were making our way along the narrow winding road to Tredannick Wartha, we heard the noise of a vehicle coming towards us. We stood to the side of the road to let it pass. As it drove by, I looked through the closed window at a horribly misshapen, grinning face staring out at us. Wide eyes – flashing teeth – a terrifying sight.

'My brothers!' cried Mortimer Tregennis, white to his lips. 'They are taking them away.'

We watched with horror as the vehicle drove slowly on. Then we continued towards the unfortunate house where some strange event had happened.

The Tregennis house was a large bright building. It had a large garden, already well-filled with spring flowers, and the window of the dining room looked out over the garden.

Holmes walked slowly and thoughtfully among the flowerbeds and along the path before we entered the house. He was so deep in thought, I remember, that he kicked a watering can by mistake, emptying the water over both our feet and the garden path.

Inside the house we were met by the housekeeper, Mrs Porter, who looked after the family. She willingly answered all Holmes's questions. She'd heard nothing in the night. Her employers had all been extremely cheerful lately. She'd fainted with horror when she first went into the room and saw that awful sight. When she recovered, she threw open the window to let in the morning air. Then she ran down to the road and sent one of the farm boys for the doctor. Miss Tregennis was on her bed upstairs if we wanted to see her. The brothers were so crazy it had taken four strong men to get them into the vehicle to take them away. Mrs Porter was not going to stay a moment longer than necessary and was leaving that very afternoon to rejoin her family.

We climbed the stairs and looked at the body. Miss Brenda Tregennis had once been beautiful. Her dark face was still attractive, even in death. However, you could see on it signs of the horror that had been her last living experience. We went back down to the dining room. In the fireplace were the ashes of last night's fire. On the table were the four burned-out candles. Cards were spread out all over its surface. The chairs had been moved back against the walls, but everything else was as it had been the night before. Holmes walked about with quick light steps. He sat in the various chairs. He moved them back where they had been the night before. He tested how much of the garden was visible. He examined the floor, the ceiling, and the fireplace. But not once did I see that sudden brightening of his eyes which would have told me that he saw some tiny piece of light in this total darkness.

'Why a fire?' he asked once. 'Did they always have a fire in this small room on a spring evening?'

Mortimer Tregennis explained that the night was cold and damp. Because of that, they lit the fire after he had arrived. 'What are you going to do now, Mr Holmes?' he asked.

'With your permission, gentlemen,' replied Holmes, 'we will now return to our cottage. It is unlikely that we will discover anything new here now. I will consider the facts, Mr Tregennis. If anything occurs to me I will certainly communicate with you and the vicar.'

It was not until long after we were back in Poldhu Cottage that Holmes broke his complete and thought-filled silence. He sat in his armchair. His face looked tired, his eyebrows pulled together in a frown. Finally he looked up and jumped to his feet.

'I don't have enough facts!' he said with a laugh. 'Let's walk along the cliffs together and search for ancient coins. We're more likely to find them than clues to this problem. The sea air, sunshine, and patience, Watson – that's what we need.

'Now, let's look calmly at our position, Watson,' he said as we walked along the cliffs. 'Let's be clear about exactly what we *do* know, so that we'll be ready to fit any fresh facts into their correct place. Firstly I hope that neither of us is prepared to believe that "the devil" is involving himself in the affairs of men. Let's begin by rejecting that idea entirely.'

Holmes paused and then continued, moving his hands as he spoke. 'That leaves three people who have been seriously and horribly affected. We can be certain about that. Now, when did this happen? Clearly, if we believe his account to be true, it was immediately after Mr Mortimer Tregennis left the room. That's a very important point. And it seems extremely likely that it was just a few minutes afterwards. The cards were still on the table. It was already past their usual hour for bed. Yet they hadn't changed their position or pushed back their chairs. I repeat, then, that the occurrence was immediately after Mr Tregennis had left, and not later than eleven o'clock last night.

'Our next obvious step is to check, as far as we can, the movements of Mortimer Tregennis after he left the room.' Holmes looked out to sea, as his explanation continued. 'There's no difficulty doing this, and he seems to be above suspicion. Knowing my methods as you do, you obviously realised why I knocked over the watering can. It was to get a better look at his footprint. It stood out clearly on the wet, sandy path. Last night was also wet, you will remember. It wasn't difficult, therefore – having once seen his footprints – to find out where he walked. He appears to have left quickly in the direction of the vicarage.

'If, then, Mortimer Tregennis disappeared from the scene,' said Holmes, stopping and looking over the cheerless countryside, 'and some outside person affected the card players, how did they cause such a scene of horror? We can cross Mrs Porter off the list. She is clearly harmless. But is there any evidence that someone came to the garden window and somehow drove everyone out of their senses?

'The only suggestion here comes from Mortimer Tregennis himself,' Holmes answered his own questions, 'who says that his brother spoke about some movement in the garden. That is certainly remarkable, as the night was rainy, cloudy, and dark. Anyone who wished to alarm these people would have to place his face right against the glass before he could be seen. There's a metre wide flowerbed outside this window, but no indication of a footprint. It's difficult to imagine, then, how someone outside the room could have achieved such a dramatic effect inside the room. And, we haven't found any possible motive. You understand our difficulties, Watson?'

'They are only too clear,' I answered truthfully.

'And yet, with a little more evidence, we may find that we can get past these problems,' said Holmes. 'So, let's put the case to one side until more accurate information is available, and we can spend the rest of our morning studying prehistoric man.'

I may have commented on my friend's extraordinary mental abilities, but never more so than on that spring morning in Cornwall. For two hours he spoke at length about ancient peoples and the way they lived, just as if there was no evil mystery waiting for him to solve.

We returned to our cottage in the afternoon and found a visitor waiting for us. Neither of us needed to be told who that visitor was. The tall, heavily-built body, the deeply-lined face with the fierce eyes, the wild grey hair, the beard, were as well known in London as in Africa. They could only belong to the huge personality of Dr Leon Sterndale, the great lion-hunter and explorer.

Between his journeys to Africa he lived on his own in a lonely cottage not far from Tredannick Wollas among his books and his maps. It was well known that he loved to keep to himself. It was a surprise to me, therefore, to hear him enthusiastically asking Holmes whether he had made any progress in solving this mystery.

'The local police are hopeless,' said Dr Sterndale, 'but perhaps your wider experience has suggested a possible explanation. I only ask because I know the Tregennis family very well. In fact, they are cousins on my mother's side of the family. These strange events have naturally been a great shock to me. In fact I'd got as far as Plymouth on my way to Africa, but the news reached me this morning, and I came straight back again to help in the inquiry.'

Holmes raised his eyebrows.

'Did you miss your boat because of it?' he asked.

'I'll take the next,' replied Sterndale.

'That's friendship indeed,' said Holmes.

'As I said, they're relatives,' said Sterndale.

'Indeed. Cousins of your mother. Was your baggage already on the ship?'

'Some of it, but the main part is at my hotel in Plymouth.'

'I see. But how did you hear the news? Surely this event could not have found its way into the Plymouth morning papers,' said Holmes.

'No, sir. I received a message,' explained Sterndale.

'Might I ask who from?' asked Holmes.

A shadow passed across the bony face of the explorer.

'You ask a lot of questions, Mr Holmes.'

'It's my business.'

With an effort Dr Sterndale recovered his previous calmness.

'Mr Roundhay, the vicar, sent me the message.'

'Thank you,' said Holmes. 'I must say that I am not completely clear about what happened. However, I have every hope of finding some answers. It's too early to say more.'

'Perhaps you could tell me if your suspicions point in any particular direction?' said Sterndale.

'No,' replied Holmes. 'I would hardly do that.'

'Then I've wasted my time,' said Sterndale suddenly and rather rudely, and hurried angrily from our cottage. Within five minutes Holmes had left too and I didn't see him again until the evening. He returned with an exhausted look on his face which told me that he had made no great progress. He looked quickly at the message waiting for him.

'From the Plymouth hotel, Watson,' he said. 'It appears that Sterndale did indeed spend last night there, and that he has actually allowed some of his baggage to go on to Africa, while he returned here. What do you make of that, Watson?'

'He's deeply interested,' I replied.

'Deeply interested. Yes,' said Holmes, a finger pressed to his lips in thought. 'There is a faint path here which we'd not yet seen and which might lead us through this jungle. Cheer up, Watson, for I'm sure that more clues will come to light.'

Little did I realise how soon Holmes would be proved right. Nor did I realise that a frightening new development would open up an entirely fresh line of investigation. I was shaving at my window in the morning when I saw the vicar throw open the garden gate and rush up our path. Holmes and I hurried downstairs to meet him.

Our visitor caught his breath and told his terrible story.

'The devil is among us, Mr Holmes!' he cried. 'Satan himself is here!' His face was sheet-white and his eyes frightened.

'Mr Mortimer Tregennis died during the night,' he said. 'And in exactly the same way as the rest of his family.'

Holmes jumped to his feet, all energy in an instant.

'Watson, we'll have breakfast later,' he said. 'Mr Roundhay, let's hurry. Hurry – before the evidence gets disturbed.'

Tregennis occupied two rooms, one above the other, at one end of the vicarage. Below was a large sitting room; above, his bedroom. They looked out over a grassy area which came up to the windows. We'd arrived before the doctor or the police, so nothing had been disturbed. The scene has left a picture in my mind which I will never be able to get rid of.

The atmosphere[27] in the room was horrible and depressing. The servant who first entered had thrown open a window. Otherwise it would have been even more unbearable. This might partly be due to the fact that a lamp was smoking in the centre of the table. Beside it sat the dead man, leaning back in his chair. His thin dark face was turned towards the window and wore the same awful expression of terror which we had seen on the face of his dead sister. His fingers were in tight fists as though he had died from sudden and uncontrollable fear. He was fully clothed, though there were signs that he'd dressed in a hurry. We learned that his bed had been slept in, and that this terrible end had come to him early in the morning.

I sensed the red-hot energy just below the surface of Holmes's calm exterior. A sudden change came over him the moment that he entered the death-filled room. Immediately he was awake and alive. His eyes shone. He was ready for activity.

He was out on the grass, in through the window, round the room, and up into the bedroom, rushing all round like a dog with its nose to the ground. In the bedroom he quickly searched the room and ended by throwing open the window. This appeared to give him fresh cause for excitement, because he leaned out of it making loud noises of interest and delight.

Then he rushed outside and threw himself down on the grass. He ran back into the room. The lamp was quite ordinary, but he examined it most carefully, taking measurements. Next he used a penknife to take off some of the black surface from the inside of the lamp. This he put into an envelope, which he placed in his wallet. Finally, just as the doctor and the police arrived, he asked me to fetch the vicar.

'I'm glad to say that my investigation has not been entirely pointless,' he said. 'I can't stay to discuss the matter with the police. But please give the inspector my best wishes. And now, Watson, I think that we'll find more to do somewhere else.'

During the next two days Holmes spent most of the time alone on country walks. He would return after many hours without a single comment as to where he'd been. One experiment[28] he made gave me a clue about his line of investigation. He bought a lamp which was exactly the same as the one in Mortimer Tregennis's room. He filled this with the same oil used at the vicarage, and he carefully worked out how much oil the lamp used when it was burning. Another experiment he made was more unpleasant, and one which I'm unlikely ever to forget.

'You will remember, Watson,' he said one afternoon, 'that there's one common point in the different reports which have reached us. In each case this concerns the effect of the atmosphere in the room on the people who first went in. Mortimer Tregennis told us that the doctor fell into a chair when he entered his brothers' dining room. Mrs Porter, the housekeeper, told us that she herself fainted when she entered the room. In the second case – the death of Mortimer Tregennis himself – remember the horrible atmosphere of the room when we arrived, even though the servant had opened the window. That servant, I discovered, was so ill afterwards that she'd gone to her bed. In each case there's evidence of a poisonous atmosphere. In each case, also, something is burning in the room: in one case a fire, in the other, a lamp. The fire was needed, but the lamp was lit – as I discovered from the amount of oil used – long after it became light in the morning. Why? Surely because there's some connection between three things: the burning, the close atmosphere, and, finally, the madness or death of these unfortunate people.'

'It would appear so,' I replied.

'It seems at least to be a likely explanation,' continued Holmes. 'Let's suppose, then, that in each case something was burned which produced an atmosphere causing strange poisonous effects. In the case of the Tregennis family this "thing" was placed in the fire. The fire would naturally carry most of the smoke up the chimney. One would therefore expect the effects of the poison to be less than in the second case, where it was more difficult for the smoke to escape. The result seems to show that this was so. In the first case only the woman was killed. The brothers showed those signs of madness, temporary or otherwise, which is obviously the first effect of the drug. The second case resulted in death. The facts, therefore, seem to suggest that a poison was used, which worked when it was burned.'

Holmes stood and looked out of the window at the sea.

'With these thoughts in my head I naturally looked about in Mortimer Tregennis's room to find some remains of this poisonous "thing",' said Holmes. 'The obvious place to look was the lamp. Sure enough, I noticed some kind of brownish powder around the edges, which had not yet been burned. As you saw, I took half of this and placed it in an envelope.'

'Why half, Holmes?' I asked.

'It's not for me, my dear Watson, to stand in the way of the police inquiry,' replied Holmes. 'I left them all the evidence I found. Now, Watson, we'll light this lamp. We will, however, open the window to avoid the unnecessarily early death of two fine individuals. You can sit near that open window in an armchair unless, like a sensible man, you decide to have nothing to do with this experiment.'

I went and sat in the armchair. Holmes smiled at me.

'I thought you'd stay,' he continued. 'I'll place my chair opposite yours, so that we may be the same distance from the poison and face to face. We'll leave the door half-open. Each of us is now in a position to watch the other and to end the experiment if the effects seem alarming. Then I take what is left of the powder from the envelope, and I put it above the burning lamp. So! Let's sit down and wait for developments.'

They were not long in coming. Almost immediately I was conscious of a sickly sweet smell. From that first moment my brain and my imagination were completely out of control.

A thick, black cloud rose before my eyes. My mind believed that this cloud contained everything in the world that was horrible and evil. Strange shapes moved and swam around. Each shape seemed like a threat or a warning of something awful about to happen, the arrival of some unspeakable evil that would destroy my mind. The storm inside my brain was such that I felt my head might break open. I tried to scream, but my voice sounded distant and far away.

At the same moment, I broke through that cloud of fearful terror and caught sight of Holmes's face. It was white, unmoving, with an expression of complete horror. It was that sight which gave me a moment of sense and of strength. I jumped from my chair, threw my arms round Holmes, and together we half-fell through the door. A moment later we had thrown ourselves face down on the grass. We lay side by side, conscious only of the wonderful sunshine burning through that awful cloud of terror. Slowly the cloud rose above us like the mist from the countryside until peace and reason returned. Eventually we sat up on the grass, our foreheads damp with sweat.

'Good God, Watson!' said Holmes at last, in a shaky voice, 'I owe you both my thanks and an apology. I shouldn't have done that experiment at all, and I certainly shouldn't have involved a friend. It was quite wrong of me. I am really very sorry.'

'You know,' I answered with some feeling, for I have never seen so much of Holmes's heart before, 'it's always an honour to help you.'

'I never imagined that the effect could be so sudden and so powerful,' said Holmes. 'Presumably, Watson, you no longer have any doubt as to how these terrible events happened?'

'None at all,' I replied.

'But the motive behind them remains as unclear as before,' said Holmes. 'Let's sit on that seat in the fresh air and discuss it. I can still taste that poisonous stuff. I think we must admit that all the evidence points to Mortimer Tregennis having been the criminal at the first event, even though he was the victim[29] at the second.

'Firstly, we must remember there's the story of a family argument, followed by a repaired friendship. How bitter that argument may have been, or how false the repaired friendship we cannot tell. But, thinking of Mortimer Tregennis, with his foxy face and the small mean eyes behind the glasses, I wouldn't judge him to be a particularly forgiving character.

'Secondly, there's the idea of someone moving in the garden. But remember that this idea came from him in the first place. He had a reason to mislead us. Finally, if he didn't throw the poison into the fire at the moment when he left the room, who did? Whatever occurred happened immediately after he left. If anyone else had come in, the family would certainly have got up from the table. Besides, in the Cornish countryside, visitors don't arrive after ten o'clock at night. We may take it, then, that all the evidence points to Mortimer Tregennis as the first criminal.'

'Then he must have killed himself!' I said excitedly.

'That's not impossible. Someone who did such a terrible thing to his own family might well feel guilty enough to do the same thing to themselves. However, there are some good reasons why this is probably not what happened. Fortunately, there's one man in England who knows all the facts, and I've made arrangements so that we can hear them directly from him. Ah! he's a little early.'

I heard the garden gate, and the huge figure of the great African explorer appeared on the path.

'Perhaps you would kindly step this way, Dr Sterndale,' Holmes called to the man. 'We've been doing an experiment indoors which has left our little room unfit to receive such an important visitor.'

Dr Sterndale turned in some surprise towards us.

'You sent for me, Mr Holmes,' said Sterndale 'and I've come, though I really don't know why I should be doing what you ask.'

'Perhaps we can clear that point up before you leave,' said Holmes. 'Meanwhile, I'm very grateful to you for coming so quickly. Please forgive this informal meeting in the open air. Perhaps also it is as well that we should talk out here where no one can hear us. The matters which we have to discuss will affect you in a very personal way.'

The explorer gave my companion a hard serious look.

'I cannot imagine, sir,' he said, 'what you can have to say that will affect me in a personal way.'

'The killing of Mortimer Tregennis,' said Holmes.

For a moment I wished that I'd had my pistol. Sterndale's fierce face turned a dark red. His eyes stared angrily. And he jumped forward raising his fists towards my companion. Then he stopped, and with a violent effort his expression took on a cold, hard calmness, which, if possible, seemed more dangerous than his anger.

'I've lived so long among wild people and beyond the law,' said he, 'that I've got into the habit of thinking I am the law. You would do well, Mr Holmes, not to forget it. I've no desire to do you an injury.'

'Nor have I any desire to do you an injury, Dr Sterndale,' replied Holmes. 'Surely the clearest proof of it is that, knowing what I know, I've sent for you and not for the police.'

'Oh!' Sterndale sat down, a shocked look on his face. Perhaps, for the first time in his adventurous life someone had won his respect. It was difficult to ignore the calm and certain power in Holmes's manner. For a moment our visitor was at a loss for words.

'If this is a bluff[30], Mr Holmes, you've chosen a bad man for your experiment,' he said. 'What do you mean?'

'I will tell you,' said Holmes. 'I hope that honesty from me will lead to honesty from you. What I do next will depend entirely on your explanation.'

'My explanation of what?' asked Sterndale.

'Your explanation of why you killed Mortimer Tregennis,' said Holmes.

Sterndale's forehead was damp with sweat.

'Do all your successes depend on an extraordinary bluff?' he asked.

'It's you who are bluffing, Dr Leon Sterndale,' said Holmes seriously. 'Not me. Let me give you some proof. I'll tell you what I believe and why. I'll give you some facts. First, you returned from Plymouth, allowing much of your baggage to go on to Africa. I'll say nothing about that except that it told me you might be involved in this drama ...'

'I came back ...' began Sterndale.

'I've heard your reasons,' Holmes interrupted, 'and I find them unlikely and insufficient. You came down here to ask me who I suspected. I refused to tell you. You then went to the vicar's house, waited outside for some time, and finally returned to your cottage.'

'How do you know that?' asked Sterndale.

'I followed you,' replied Holmes.

'I saw no one,' said Sterndale.

'That's what you may expect when I follow you,' replied Holmes. 'You spent a restless night and you made plans. Then, leaving your cottage as the sun was coming up, you filled your pocket with some reddish stones that were lying beside your gate.'

Sterndale stared at Holmes in amazement.

'You then walked quickly to the vicar's house. You were wearing, I can tell you, the same pair of shoes which are on your feet at the moment. At the house you made your way through the trees, coming out under Tregennis's window. It was now daylight, but the household was not yet stirring. You took some of the stones from your pocket, and threw them up at the window above you.'

Sterndale jumped to his feet.

'You're the devil himself!' he cried.

Holmes smiled at the praise. 'It took two, or possibly three, handfuls of stones before the lodger came to the window. You waved to him to come down. He dressed hurriedly and came down to his sitting room. You went in through the window. There was a brief conversation. Then you left and closed the window. You stood outside, watching what happened through the window. Finally, when Tregennis was dead, you returned the way you had come. Now, Dr Sterndale, how do you explain such behaviour, and what were the motives for your actions? Do not hide the truth and do not try and trick me. Otherwise, I promise you, the matter will pass from my hands to those of the police.'

Our visitor's face had turned grey as he listened to the words of his accuser. He sat in thought for some time with his face sunk in his hands. Then with a sudden movement he pulled a photograph from his pocket and threw it on the table.

'That's why,' he said.

The photo showed the face of a very beautiful woman. Holmes bent over it.

'Brenda Tregennis,' he said.

'Yes, Brenda Tregennis,' repeated our visitor. 'For years I loved her. For years she loved me. That's the secret of why I hide myself away in Cornwall. People wonder why I come here. The truth is simple. It brought me close to the one thing on earth that was dear to me. I could not marry her because I already have a wife. She left me years ago, but I was not able to divorce her. For years Brenda waited. For years I waited. And just look how it's all ended.' Sterndale gave a great cry and threw up his hands. Then with an effort he became calm again and continued:

'The vicar knew,' continued Sterndale. 'He was in our confidence. He'll tell you that she was a truly wonderful person. That was why he sent me the message. My baggage was of no importance to me. Nor Africa. Not when I heard about what had happened. There you have the missing clue, the explanation for my actions, Mr Holmes.'

'Go on,' said my friend.

Dr Sterndale took a paper packet from his pocket and put it on the table. On the outside was written in Latin '*Radix pedis diaboli*' with 'poison' in red writing beneath it. He pushed it towards me. 'I understand that you are a doctor, sir. Have you ever heard of this?'

'Devil's-foot root[31]!' I translated from the Latin. 'No, I've never heard of it.'

'That in no way means that your professional knowledge is at fault,' said Sterndale. 'I believe I'm the only person in Europe to have any. You can't find it in any textbooks on medicines or poisons. It gets its name because the root is shaped like a foot: half human, half goat. It's used by the medicine men in certain parts of West Africa. I got this in the Ubangi country.'

He opened the paper as he spoke and showed us a quantity of reddish-brown powder.

'Go on, sir,' said Holmes, a serious look on his face.

'Don't worry. I'll tell you everything, Mr Holmes,' continued Sterndale. 'I've already explained my relationship with the Tregennis family. Because of my relationship with the sister I was friendly with the brothers. There was a family argument about money. As a result, Mortimer left the family home. Some time later, they sorted out the problem and were all supposedly friends again. But Mortimer was a clever, nasty, mean man. Several things happened which caused me to be suspicious of him. Though I never had cause for any open disagreement.'

Sterndale paused, looking from Holmes to me and back again.

'A few weeks ago,' he went on. 'Mortimer Tregennis came down to my cottage and I showed him some of the interesting things I'd brought back from Africa. Among other things I showed him this powder, and I told him of its strange effect. I explained how it reaches that part of the brain which controls fear and how it causes madness or death. I also told him how it would be impossible for European science to tell that it had been used. There's no doubt that's when he took it. I never left the room, but I was opening cupboards and bending down to open boxes. He must have managed to steal some of the devil's-foot root when I wasn't looking. He asked me many questions about the amount and the time that was needed for it to take effect. I never dreamed that he could have a personal reason for asking.

'I thought no more about it until the vicar's message reached me. The evil Tregennis obviously thought that I'd be at sea before the news reached me. But I returned at once. Of course, once I heard the details I knew that my poison had been used. I came round to see if you had another explanation. But there could be none. I was certain that Mortimer Tregennis was the murderer. I was sure that he'd done it for the money. Perhaps he thought that if the other members of his family were all mad he could look after their joint property. He'd driven two of them out of their senses. And he'd killed his sister Brenda, the one person I've ever loved and who has ever loved me. That was his crime. What was to be his punishment?

'I couldn't go to the police. What proof did I have? Revenge was everything to me. I told you once before, Mr Holmes, that I've started to believe that I am the law. That's how it is. I decided that what Tregennis had done to others should be done to him.

'Now I've told you everything. You know the rest. As you rightly worked out, I threw the stones up at his window. He came down and let me in. I told him that I'd come both to judge him and to carry out the sentence. The rat sank into a chair, frozen at the sight of my gun. I lit the lamp and put the powder in it. Then I stood outside the window, ready to shoot him if he tried to leave the room. He died within five minutes. My God, how he died! But my heart was hard as stone. He suffered nothing which my dear Brenda had not felt before him. That's my story, Mr Holmes. Perhaps, if you loved a woman, you'd have done much the same as I did. Anyway, I'm in your hands. There's no man alive who can fear death less than I do at the present moment.'

Holmes sat for some time in silence.

'What were your plans?' he asked at last.

'I'd intended to return to central Africa. My work there is but half finished.'

'Go and do the other half,' said Holmes. 'I, at least, am not prepared to prevent you.'

Dr Sterndale stood up slowly, looking at Holmes with curiosity. Then he walked from the garden. Holmes sat back and looked out to sea.

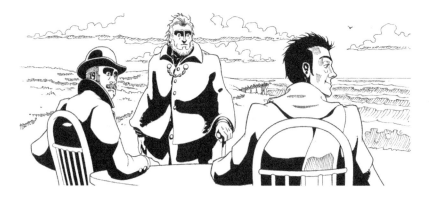

'I think you must agree, Watson,' he said, 'that this is not a case which we need to get involved with any further. Our investigation has been independent, and our action will be independent too. Would you give this man up to the police?'

'Certainly not,' I answered.

'I have never loved, Watson,' said Holmes. But if I had, and if the woman I loved had been killed like that, I might even do what our lawless lion-hunter has done. Who knows? Well, Watson, I will not show disrespect for your intelligence by explaining what is obvious. The stones on the grass by the window were, of course, the first clue. They were unlike anything in the vicar's garden. Only when my attention had been drawn to Dr Sterndale and his cottage did I find some similar stones. The lamp still shining in the daylight and the remains of powder were two more events that formed a fairly obvious chain. And now, my dear Watson, I think we may put the matter out of our minds. My work is done. I can return with an untroubled mind to the study of the ancient Cornish language.'

ACTIVITIES

• •

1 Check your answers to *Before you read* on page 76.

2 Put the events in order.

1 Mortimer Tregennis is found dead. ☐
2 Holmes and Watson visit the Tregennis house. ☐
3 Mortimer Tregennis argues with his family about money. ☐
4 Holmes follows Sterndale to the vicar's house. ☐
5 The local vicar and Mortimer Tregennis visit Holmes and Watson in their cottage. ☐
6 Mortimer Tregennis plays cards with his sister and brothers. ☐
7 Leon Sterndale returns from Plymouth to Cornwall. ☐
8 Brenda Tregennis is found dead. ☐
9 Holmes does an experiment with a lamp. ☐
10 Mortimer Tregennis steals some devil's-foot root. ☐

3 Read the sentences and write T (true) or F (false).

1 Holmes goes to Cornwall on holiday to relax. ☐
2 Brenda dies shortly after Mortimer leaves the house. ☐
3 Mrs Porter thinks the Tregennis family had been arguing. ☐
4 Holmes thinks someone has been standing outside the dining room window of the Tregennis house. ☐
5 Leon Sterndale has just returned from Africa. ☐
6 Leon Sterndale read in the newspaper that Brenda Tregennis was dead. ☐
7 A servant finds the body of Mortimer Tregennis. ☐
8 Holmes takes something from the lamp in Mortimer Tregennis's sitting room. ☐

4 Which evidence does Sherlock Holmes use to solve the case?

1 a poisonous atmosphere ☐
2 a lamp burning ☐
3 red stones ☐
4 ancient coins ☐
5 a photograph of Brenda Tregennis ☐
6 a textbook about medicines and poisons ☐
7 a gun ☐
8 a watering can ☐

5 Answer the questions.

1 Why does Mortimer Tregennis kill Brenda Tregennis?

2 Why does Leon Sterndale kill Mortimer Tregennis?

3 Why does Holmes let Leon Sterndale walk away?

6 Now think about all three stories and answer the questions.

1 Which story did you like best? Why?

2 Which story did you like least? Why?

3 What have you found out about the character of Sherlock Holmes? Do you like him? Why / why not?

Glossary

[1]**telegram** (page 6) *noun*   an old fashioned kind of message

[2]**inquest** (page 9) *noun*   an investigation into how someone died

[3]**Woolwich Arsenal** (page 9) *place*   the place where weapons were made for the British army and navy

[4]**technical** (page 10) *adjective*   to do with the practical use of machines, etc.

[5]**Scotland Yard** (page 10) *place*   the central office for the police in London

[6]**submarine** (page 12) *noun*   a ship that goes under water

[7]**navy** (page 12) *noun*   the warships of a country

[8]**safe** (page 12) *noun*   a strong metal box or cupboard with a lock

[9]**points** (page 17) *noun*   a place where two railway lines join each other

[10]**carriages** (page 18) *noun*   separate parts of a train for carrying passengers

[11]**servant** (page 20) *noun*   a person who works in someone's house cooking, cleaning, etc.

[12]**cosh** (page 41) *noun*   a short thick heavy stick used as a weapon

[13]**governess** (page 46) *noun*   an old-fashioned term for a woman employed to teach the children of a rich family

[14]**egotism** (page 47) *noun*   thinking you are better than everyone else

[15]**whim** (page 52) *noun*   a sudden, and often unusual, wish

[16]**chestnut** (page 52) *adjective*   a dark reddish brown colour

[17]**skylight** (page 64) *noun*   a window in the roof

[18]**cellar** (page 66) *noun*   a room below ground

[19]**ladder** (page 69) *noun*   a piece of equipment used to climb up to (for example) a high window

[20]**will** (page 71) *noun*   a document that says what will happen to a person's property etc. when they die

[21]**vicar** (page 76) *noun*   a religious man or woman in charge of an Anglican church

[22]**Cornwall** (page 78) *place*   the far south-west of Britain

[23]**cliffs** (page 78) *noun*   a high, steep area of rock

[24]**lodger** (page 79) *noun*   a person who pays rent to live in someone's house

[25]**candle** (page 81) *noun*   a stick of wax that burns to give light

[26]**devil** (page 84) *noun*   the most powerful evil being

[27]**atmosphere** (page 94) *noun*   the air in a room or a small space

[28]**experiment** (page 95) *noun*   a scientific test

[29]**victim** (page 98) *noun*   a person who is attacked or injured

[30]**bluff** (page 101) *noun*   an attempt to trick someone

[31]**root** (page 103) *noun*   the part of a plant that grows under the ground